Everyday Dress of Rural America
1783–1800

With Instructions and Patterns

Merideth Wright

Illustrated by Nancy Rexford

Dover Publications, Inc.

New York

To my husband, Frederic Emigh,
my son Aren and my daughter Sophie

Made possible in part by a grant from
the Vermont Statehood Bicentennial Commission.

Text and diagrams copyright © 1990, 1992 by Merideth Wright.
Illustrations copyright © 1990 by Nancy Rexford.
All rights reserved under Pan American and International Copyright
Conventions.

Published in Canada by General Publishing Company, Ltd., 30 Lesmill Road,
Don Mills, Toronto, Ontario.
Published in the United Kingdom by Constable and Company, Ltd., 3 The
Lanchesters, 162–164 Fulham Palace Road, London W6 9ER.

This Dover edition, first published in 1992, is an unabridged republication of
Put On Thy Beautiful Garments: Rural New England Clothing, 1783–1800,
first published by The Clothes Press, East Montpelier, VT, in 1990 under
ISBN: 0-9625656-0-1. Slight corrections have been made to this edition, and
some material has been updated.

Manufactured in the United States of America.
Dover Publications, Inc., 31 East 2nd Street, Mineola, N.Y. 11501

Library of Congress Cataloging-in-Publication Data

Wright, Merideth.
    Everyday dress of rural America, 1783–1800 : with instructions and pat-
terns / Merideth Wright ; illustrated by Nancy Rexford.
        p.   cm.
    Corrected and updated ed. of: Put on thy beautiful garments. East
Montpelier, Vt. : Clothes Press, c1990.
    Includes bibliographical references.
    ISBN 0-486-27320-2
    1. Costume—New England—History—18th century. 2. New
England—Social life and customs. 3. Dressmaking—Patterns.
I. Wright, Merideth. Put on thy beautiful garments. II. Title.
GT617.N28W74   1992
391'.00974'09033—dc20
                                                    92-39106
                                                      CIP

Acknowledgments

Now I understand what authors mean when they say that the people they want to thank are "too numerous to mention!" I would particularly like to thank Vermont's State Librarian, Patricia Klinck, and the Director of the Vermont Historical Society, Michael Sherman, for encouraging me to persist in this project and to submit it to the Vermont Statehood Bicentennial Commission for its support, and Carolyn Meub of the Commission for adding her personal interest and ideas; Nancy Rexford, who as both a friend and colleague shares the innate excitement of turning up new tidbits of costume information, and who has done a superb job of illustrating this book; printer Bob Sharp for encouraging me to think this book might be possible after all; Mary Labate Rogstad for helping me to study items in the Vermont Historical Society collection; Gordon Day for sharing a set of drawings of traditional Western Abenaki clothing rendered from his research notes spanning twenty years; Marilyn Blackwell for introducing me to Mary Palmer Tyler, the subject of her master's thesis; the Vermont Department of Libraries reference staff who entered into the spirit of my frequent and very odd requests; the museum staff at the many other museums I visited and at the more numerous museums I wrote to for slides; the people who took the time to read the manuscript and respond with their thoughtful comments: Barbara Floersch, Larry Floersch, and Jessica Nicoll; and Eleanor Ott, Jeanne Brink and Fred Wiseman who helped me to include the Western Abenaki in this book. In a wonderful coincidence, Larry Copp, who generously spent his time and knowledge providing computer typesetting, is a member of the Connecticut family whose collection of linen garments given to the Smithsonian appears in the bibliography. I also want to thank Ben Bergstein and April Werner of the Green Mountain Volunteers traditional New England dance group, for originally setting me the task of figuring out what people in Vermont wore; my mother, Betty Wright, who said, "You should write a book!"; and three people from whom I must have inherited this curiosity about what people wore and how it was made: my grandfather David Greenhouse, an expert cutter in the garment industry, my grandmother Yetta Greenhouse, who taught me to sew, and my father, Oscar Wright, an industrial arts teacher, who taught me a love of fine hand work in many fields.

The errors and omissions in this book are, alas, all my own.

Foreword

In third grade I read a book about a boy growing up in Williamsburg, Virginia, in the mid 1700s. I have forgotten the title and all but a few episodes of the story, but I remember vividly the description of what the boy wore in town, on a river expedition, and at a formal occasion; and I recall how the description of his clothing fired my imagination; how much I wished I could wear clothing like that. When, soon afterward, a well-meaning relative gave me a "Hopalong Cassidy" cowboy hat, I refashioned it with safety pins into a tricorne, and when my parents took me to Williamsburg, I remember the sense of familiarity I had because of the clothing the guides wore — it was just like the book I had read.

A few years later, for some unaccountable reason, Civil War military caps became all the rage among schoolchildren. At about the same time, thanks to Walt Disney, coonskin caps became indispensible articles of playtime headgear. All of these bits and pieces of "historical" costume made their way into my childhood collection of essential possessions and contributed to my childhood awareness of the past as different from my ordinary life, but familiar and connected to it.

I report these episodes because they are typical of the way many of us make contact with the past. As any museum curator can attest, the "try-on" corner is often the busiest part of the galleries, crowded with children working themselves into adult-sized clothing from another era while adults hover at the fringe, experiencing — mostly vicariously — this special kind of historical consciousness, and occasionally venturing into the action to get the feel of fabrics and fashions from the past.

Merideth Wright gives us yet another pathway into the past by describing the clothing worn in the 1790s by Abenakis, by well-to-do inhabitants of the settled New England towns and villages, and by settlers in the rural and frontier areas of the new state of Vermont. Nancy Rexford's drawings complement the text with visual details that show us how the many layers of eighteenth-century clothing looked, were worn, and worked together. Wright and Rexford go further, however, and give us information about construction and materials that allows us to understand how clothing defined and was defined by social class and demeanor, how it conformed to and restricted the activities for which it was designed and in which it was used.

This book is a work of true scholarship. Wright and Rexford have garnered information from letters, diaries, newspapers, and other primary sources. They also have first-hand knowledge of garments from the period: each has handled, examined, and analyzed many eighteenth-century garments to understand the construction, sewing techniques, and materials of the period. The result of their research is a deep appreciation of the social, economic, cultural, and political implications of clothing. We learn how Abenakis and the newer settlers borrowed materials and garments from each other; how Americans began defining a style of their own, distinct from

European fashion that prevailed in previous generations; and how the expanding networks of communication, commerce, and industry within the new United States and between the United States and a wider world affected what people wore in New England at the end of the eighteenth century.

This way of studying clothing will help us understand the 1790s in Vermont and the northeast a little better. It will also help us understand our own time a little better, for a close reading of this book will give us technical information and a method for examining and analyzing the garments we wear in our own time. And some readers will get even more enjoyment from this book as they try their hands at recreating garments from the 1790s using the pattern diagrams, instructions, and information about appropriate fabrics and resources.

As Vermonters prepare to celebrate the bicentennial of the state's union with the United States in 1791, we are learning new facts about material life, social and economic organization, and the many ways Vermont was already tied to the wider political and cultural world around it. This book about what people wore then, who wore what, and how clothing was made and remade to suit changing fashions in the early years of statehood is a valuable contribution to what we can know about the past. It gives us another chance to connect with that curiosity we felt as children trying on clothing of another era. It extends the range of our historical imagination, which is the key to historical understanding.

Michael Sherman

Director, Vermont Historical Society

Preface

The clothing worn by people of a given time and place is one of the most intimate expressions of their culture. Because we all wear some sort of clothing of our own time and place, we have a reference point from which to reach out, both to compare others' clothing with our own, and to imagine ourselves in their place. Clothing is primarily a familiar part of our daily social lives, rather than a manifestation of political or economic history. It is not surprising that the metaphor for truly understanding other people is to put yourself "in their shoes."

As well as carrying the freight of imagination, clothing also has a purely tactile appeal. People have a hard time resisting the urge to reach out and touch displayed clothing as a means of experiencing it fully — much to the dismay of museum curators the world around. But we cannot indulge that urge to wear or use the old pieces of clothing which have been saved down the years in attics or in museums. They are a non-renewable resource and we should not deprive future generations of a piece of their cultural heritage. By making reproductions of old garments, using the fabrics and construction methods that were used to make the originals, we can experience the clothing of other times and cultures, while preserving original pieces for the future.

In many ways understanding what daily life was like for people of another time is just as difficult as understanding and appreciating what life is like for people of a different culture and heritage in the present day. Many things turn out to be more familiar than expected, some things are surprisingly different, and some of the differences are surprisingly important.

This book is for anyone who likes simply to read and think about life in other places, times, and cultures. It is also written for those who are working at bridging the gap from imagination to experience by dressing in the appropriate clothing to do the dances, or prepare and spin and weave the flax or wool, or sing the songs, or tan the hides, or cook and eat the food, or work out the military maneuvers, or hunt, or fish, or do any number of things as they were done in another time or are done in another culture today. To take the time and make the effort to learn how it was or is "really" done shows a welcome respect for the other place, time or culture. Such respect is the foundation for a true understanding of both of the hard work and the beauty inherent in another way of life, and I will be very satisfied if this book in any way helps to increase the store of respect and understanding in today's world.

East Montpelier, Vermont   February, 1990.

Table of Contents

Part 1

What People Wore

Setting the Stage

How do we know what people wore?
Terminology and references
Using this book for making reproductions of clothing

Fashionable Clothing in the Established Towns

Clothing in the New Settlements

Clothing of the Western Abenaki

A Word About Children's Clothing

Setting the Stage

This book tells some of the story of what people in the northeast United States wore two hundred years ago. It is not the story of English or French fashion, or even of high fashion as it was known in Boston or New York. Rather, it is the story of the adoption and adaptation of clothing styles in inland and northern New England in the years between the end of the American Revolution and the turn of the nineteenth century.

Within these geographical limits, there is more focus on Vermont, because the initial impetus for this research came from the interest in Vermont in clothing appropriate for celebrating the bicentennial of its admission to the federal union as a state in 1791. That year Royall Tyler told his future wife that he was going to Vermont, "then considered the outskirts of creation by many, and where all the rogues and runaways congregated, and for that reason considered a good place for lawyers" (Tyler, 151). For Vermont, statehood in 1791 was a key to an increase in immigration, largely from the other New England states, notably Connecticut and to some extent Massachusetts. The newcomers were largely of European background (mostly English), but also included free black settlers, such as Ichabod and Mary Twilight who settled in Bradford, Vermont in 1792 (Hileman, 6; B. Smith, 20).

This is not the book to tell the history of inland New England in the late eighteenth century, nor to explore the relationships among the native Americans and the settlers from southern and coastal New England. For the purposes of examining what people wore, it is sufficient to know that the Western Abenaki were the original inhabitants of this region and continued to live there (Moody, 58-59), that many people from southern and eastern New England were emigrating to establish homesteads and new villages, and that some substantial towns were already well established.

Throughout this book, items of traditional Western Abenaki clothing are presented together with the equivalent settlers' clothing, according to their function. The limited amount of information available to me during the research for this book made it impossible for this book to contain as much detail about the Abenaki clothing as it deserves, and measured patterns for their construction and decoration are not provided. Perhaps more specific information can be published some day by the Abenaki cultural center which is now in the planning stages.

This book first presents the combinations of clothing typically worn in the established towns, in the newer settlements, and by the Western Abenaki towards the end of the eighteenth century. It then takes a closer look at each individual item of clothing with more information on how it was made and worn and the range of variations in style and materials. Part 3 provides information on fabrics and sewing techniques, Part 4 refers the reader to sources of materials, patterns, and more information, and Part 5 is a bibliography of published material, and lists museum holdings of some relevant paintings and costume pieces.

How do we know what people wore?

There are many sources for determining what people wore. Each source has its problems, but by cross-checking the different types of information it is possible to get a fair idea of what was actually worn and used in rural New England as the eighteenth century drew to a close. New research, of course, is always turning up new information.

Clothing pieces themselves are the best evidence, when it is known who wore them and when they were worn. Catalogues of museum exhibitions are often good sources of information on actual clothing. But items of clothing for which the wearer and date are documented are extremely rare, even in larger museum collections. Even if it is known who wore a piece and when that person lived, unless the garment is a wedding dress or was worn to a dated occasion such as an inauguration, the year it was worn is rarely known. Sometimes clothing comes into a collection or is passed down in a family or community with oral traditions about who wore it or when it was made. These stories are valuable and should be recorded — they may be the only information available about the piece or the method of construction. What is necessary is to see whether the stories are consistent with other known facts about the clothing's style and materials.

Writings of contemporaries are useful sources — both diaries or letters written at the time and travel writings and reminiscences written for posterity and published at a later date. It is important to keep in mind the author's point of view, allowing for the selective hindsight and ethnocentrism sometimes found when people describe their personal past or describe another group or culture. In well-established areas, newspaper advertisements occasionally give brief and tantalizing descriptions of stolen clothing, the clothing of runaway apprentices or the stock of newly opened tailor's shops or dry goods stores. Inventories in the probate records may also be useful, although those records only show what a person owned when he or she died, not what year it was worn or was fashionable.

Contemporary portraits may be a good source for information, although only for the best clothing of the people who could afford to commission portraits, and then only if the portrait painter did not take artistic license with the clothing. The famous British painter Sir Joshua Reynolds cautioned portrait painters not to paint their subjects in modern dress, warning that its very familiarity would breed contempt. He recommended that they paint their figures dressed in "something with the general air of the antique for the sake of dignity," while preserving something of the modern "for the sake of likeness" (Reynolds, 1220). It is dangerous to draw any conclusions on contemporary dress from portraits showing the sitter in a generic, artfully draped gown, betraying no idea of how it was fastened or other prosaic details. Unfortunately for research into costume history, very few American painters at the end of the eighteenth century portrayed scenes of everyday life ("genre" scenes), which might have shown what ordinary people wore.

There is little to be said about secondary sources. Some are very good, some are not reliable or are only reliable in spots. In older writings it is hard to determine the basis of the original research and thus whether the information being passed along is reliable or presents an overly romantic view of the past. Some books contain valuable descriptions of actual documented pieces that were in private collections and are now no longer available for study. Others drew their conclusions indiscriminately from portraits, with the problems already noted.

Terminology and references

This book uses the terms for fabric and clothing pieces that were used in the 1790s, explaining them in the text. Certain terms have gone out of use (e.g., "stays," "stock," or "lustring"). Some clothing pieces had other names in the nineteenth century before going out of use in the present day (e.g., "chemise," "corset," or "fichu"). Yet other terms are still in use but have changed their meaning (e.g., "petticoat" or "calico"). It is altogether too confusing to switch back and forth among the different terms from the eighteenth, nineteenth and twentieth centuries.

Parenthetical references to sources are used because they occupy less room in the text but still allow reasonably easy access to the primary sources. Sources for quotations and specific statements are given in parentheses in the text, showing the author's name and the page number, or the artist's name and the title of the work. The full entry for each source is found in the bibliography. Thus, Sarah Emery's description of the emigration of her aunt and uncle from Newburyport, Massachusetts to Berlin, Vermont in 1795 is given by the reference: (Emery, 22). Books and works of art not cited for specific examples are listed only in the bibliography, which also contains a section listing costume pieces in museum collections.

Using this book for making reproductions of clothing

Lest the prospect of making any of the clothes described in this book seems too daunting, consider the experience of young Mary Palmer when visiting her aunt and uncle just over the western Massachusetts border in New Lebanon, New York, in the summer of 1792:

> Aunt came into the sitting room, where I had been setting things in order, bringing in a whole piece of linen which looked as if it had just been boiled out, ready for sewing, and said in her cheerful manner, "Here, dear, I have brought you linen, it is to make shirts for your uncle; here is one to measure by and you may be all summer making them, if you like."
> "I shall like to do them very much,' said I, 'when will you cut them out?"
> "Oh, you must cut them out yourself, I am very busy preparing to move."
> "Oh my dear aunt! I never cut out a shirt in my life. I dare not do it."

"Fiddle-de-de," said she, "there must be a first time, and you may as well begin now as ever. A young woman is not fit to be married until she can make a shirt."

"But I never cut out one, I fear I shall spoil the linen."

"I'll venture that; cut out one and make it, we shall see."

So saying she left the room to my dismay; but I was too proud not to try, and went to work resolutely, and made out bravely, so that, before I left there, I made the six shirts, besides all my playing and riding, and had the credit besides of doing them very well" (Tyler, 175-76).

In many households all the clothes were made at home, while in others an itinerant tailor came around to sew at least the men's and boys' clothing. Some families also had a dressmaker in to sew the women's clothes, or at least to do the cutting and remodeling of those clothes (Goodrich, 74; Emery, 9 and 47; Wells, F., 142).

The characteristics of eighteenth-century garment construction are the absence of darts and the use of gussets (square or triangular inserts of cloth), gathering, or pleating. If close fit was wanted it was accomplished with curved seams (as in the back of the coat, and waistcoat, the gown bodice, and the stays). If roomy fit was needed it was accomplished with gussets (as in the shirt and shift), gathering (as in the shirt and breeches), pleating (as in the petticoat and gown), and drawstrings (as in the muslin chemise gown). Many garments were lined, usually with a medium weight plain-woven linen, but sometimes with pieces of plain or printed cotton.

The pattern diagrams in this book are all given at a scale of one square equals one inch or two squares equal five centimeters. (This book has the misfortune to be written while the United States is undecided which of the two systems to favor.) The diagrams do NOT provide a seam allowance; seam allowances must be added when planning out the pieces. In any event, the pattern pieces must be adjusted for the size of the person for whom the garment is being made. For loose garments that is not very difficult, but for the gown bodice and men's coat, vest, and breeches, with curved seams, a muslin or non-woven fabric mock-up should be made first. An old sheet may be used, or a commercial "pattern tracer" material is sold for this purpose. At least one brand, called "Tru-Grid," is available printed with one-inch squares to help in enlarging pattern diagrams. For more information, see Hunnisett or Johnson.

The pattern diagrams can be enlarged onto tissue paper or onto brown paper bags as our grandmothers used to do. I use an inexpensive paper, slightly stiffer than commercial pattern tissue, which is sold in art or drafting supply stores to architects and builders. It is available in rolls 24 inches wide by 50 feet long, which should last anyone through many projects. Garments that are made of rectangles of fabric, such as the shift, petticoat, or shirt, can just be measured and cut along the grain of the fabric, but make sure that the dimensions are right for the person who will wear it.

How to fit a pattern to a particular person is beyond the scope of this book. There are many books available in libraries and bookstores on fitting and altering patterns. In a nutshell, the rule is to keep the shapes of the pattern pieces correct while enlarging or reducing them. The way to do this is to measure the person being fitted and to compare that measurement with the corresponding measurement of the pattern pieces to find out how many inches (or centimeters) must be added or subtracted to make the garment fit. Divide that amount evenly among the pattern pieces, then cut each pattern piece apart in the middle, along the straight grain of the pattern either top to bottom, side to side, or both. Then spread the pieces apart or overlap them, until enough has been added or subtracted for the person being fitted.

While there are no full-size patterns commercially available that are altogether correct for the narrow time period covered by this book, several companies make patterns which are usable as a starting point, bearing in mind that they may need to be adapted in some way. These companies are listed in Part 4. Full-size paper patterns as known today were not in general use until the 1870s. Earlier in the nineteenth century reduced-size diagrams such as the ones in this book were provided in fashion magazines or tailors' trade magazines. In the 1790s cutting and styling information was transmitted by descriptive letters, fashion plates, miniature garments made for dressmakers' dolls, and by copying actual garments, as Mary Palmer had to do.

Fashionable Clothing in the Established Towns

By concluding a war for political independence from Great Britain, the American colonists did not also suddenly become independent of European style and culture. Fashionable Americans had inherited the eighteenth century European ideal of elegance and graceful ease, and it took some time for American fashion to develop a distinct style. A widely travelled gentleman visiting Boston in 1792 remarked that he did not think there was "another city in the world where one would meet" so many "beautiful and elegantly dressed" women as those attending the dancing assemblies (Cutting, 65). This easy elegance was emulated, if not always achieved, in smaller established towns as well.

By the mid-eighteenth century, European and colonial fashion had achieved an elegant control of dress and body carriage by limiting flexibility from the hips to the shoulders with men's tight hip-length waistcoats and women's long stays (corsets). These styles slowly evolved, so that by the late 1780s the fashionable men's waistcoat and the waistline of women's stays and gowns were at the natural waist, making more freedom of movement possible.

A fashionable man would not have been seen in public in his shirtsleeves. To be fully dressed was to wear a suit of clothes: knee-length breeches, silk stockings, a waistcoat, and a coat (the equivalent of a suit coat in a modern man's suit). A fashionable woman's dress was some variety of a gown, with a very low-cut neckline, usually filled in by a bouffant gauzy kerchief. The skirts of the gown were often cut to fall open in the front, so that a matching or contrasting petticoat would show. A fashionable woman's posture was somewhat tipped forward, emphasizing the bouffant neck-kerchief in front and the pleated and perhaps padded upper part of the skirts in the back.

In the decades after the Revolution, clothing styles in Europe became generally simpler, and only clothing meant to be worn at the royal courts remained elaborately decorated. Fashionable Americans also saw the less highly decorated styles of dress as reflecting an ideal of sobriety and industriousness befitting their great experiment in self-government. Even the most ceremonial of American men's suits were not heavily embroidered, although they often were decorated with enormous buttons. In 1789, George Washington's inaugural suit was remarkably plain, described as a "citizen's dress, the cloth of American manufacture, of a dark brown color; I believe the whole . . . alike" (Tyler, 120).

The 1790s saw a gradual shortening of the waistline for both men and women, and a change to fine, soft white cotton fabrics for fashionable women's dresses. These gowns at first retained the natural waistline and earlier gown design, but were soon constructed more simply, with a drawstring neck and waistline, and decorated by a wide sash (often pink or light blue). By 1800 fashionable American women were wearing high-waisted, columnar, white gowns, meant to evoke ancient Greek statuary. This change in fashion met with some objections, but caught on despite its unsuitability to the New England climate. Congregationalist minister Timothy Dwight, president of Yale College, advised in 1811 that "A young lady dressed à la Grecque in a New-England winter violates alike good sense, correct taste, sound morals, and the duty of self-preservation" (quoted in Fennelly [Garb], 5). Of course, the older styles were retained longer in the more rural areas of New England, and by older and more conservative people (Weeks, 295). However, inland and northern New England was not as isolated as one might think, and the new styles became current soon enough throughout the region.

Clothing in the New Settlements

After the American Revolution, and especially after the land disputes in Vermont were resolved, there was an increase in emigration from coastal and southern New England to the northern mountain valleys. These emigrants faced a life in which fashionable silk gowns and coats were of little use. Even in the well-established towns, such finery would be saved for Sunday best, and for most people, printed cotton gowns and fine broadcloth coats were their best clothing. Workday clothes were normally made of home-manufactured linen or woolen cloth, dyed with butternut bark or indigo. In places that boasted fulling mills or clothiers' establishments, such homespun woolen cloth could be given a more professional finish and more uniform dye job than could be done at home.

Not only did back-country settlers choose different fabrics for their clothes than they had worn in the cities and towns, but they also chose to wear some different garments. In 1792, Mary Palmer was surprised to find her aunt, in New Lebanon, New York, dressed in clothing that even the servants back home in Boston would not "be seen in of an afternoon." Her aunt wore a black wool petticoat and a calico apron and shortgown, with a muslin handkerchief crossed over her bosom and pinned (Tyler, 160). Many women who emigrated, such as Bathsheba Walker Goldsbury, brought their calico gowns from the Connecticut and Massachusetts towns from which they had moved (Fenwick, 3-4). Mrs. Davis of Montpelier, Vermont actually brought a silk one (Thompson, 76). For everyday wear, however, they wore the homespun woolen flannel and checked linen gowns and aprons made in their own households.

Men dressed "as plain or plainer" than the women, wearing rough linen "tow" cloth in summer, striped homespun woolens for winter, and having perhaps one good suit of homespun wool cloth which had been professionally finished and dyed (Thompson, 77). The fashionable coat was impractical for farm work, and many men wore a "frock," shaped like an oversized shirt and made of linen or wool, over their clothing when working.

Sarah Emery of Newburyport, Massachusetts remembered the excitement when her aunt and uncle emigrated to Berlin, Vermont in 1795, and how the whole family and neighborhood helped to give them a good start. "Clothing for a year or two in advance must be prepared. One sister cut a generous quarter from her web of linen; another from her fulled cloth; . . . another relative gave cloth for woolen dresses, and stocking yarn . . . . There was a round of farewell visits, each of which was turned into a sewing-bee for the benefit of the emigrants" (Emery, 22).

But it would be a mistake to think of even the most remote areas as totally isolated. A brisk trade in goods, produce, and information, including visits back to the family home in Connecticut or Massachusetts, kept even the more remote settlements advised of styles and other news, even if it might be some months out of date. And there was great demand for people skilled at remodeling clothes in the newer styles (Emery, 47).

Clothing of the Western Abenaki

The Abenaki (the people of the Dawnland or of the East) are the Native American group historically inhabiting northern and inland New England and the St. Lawrence river valley in Canada. Their traditional clothing was made of soft tanned deerskin or moose hide, sometimes decorated with dyes or with complex embroidery of dyed porcupine quills and moose hair (Calloway, 32-33).

By the end of the eighteenth century, the Abenaki had experienced more than two centuries of involvement with French, English, and Dutch traders and colonists, renting land to them, teaching them woodland survival skills, serving as guides, trading with them, caught up in fighting with them and against them, and intermarrying (at least with the French). Every aspect of their lives, including their clothing, was affected by this interaction (Moody, 58-59). For example, certain materials, such as the dense woolen blue or red "trade cloth" and European glass beads, were added to the inventory of materials from which the Abenaki made and decorated their clothing.

All the inhabitants of the new United States — native Americans, former European colonists, and former Africans — were changed by the experience of the early days of the new nation, as they had already been changed by the colonial experience on this continent. With the exception of certain religious sects, no group dressed uniformly; there has always been wide variation in clothing depending on individual wealth, taste, and devotion to tradition. This book can convey only a suggestion of what might have been typical of Abenaki clothing in the late eighteenth century, already affected by the availability of European cloth, trade shirts, and glass beads, but not yet relegated to a largely ceremonial role in Abenaki life.

The basic garment for men was a breechcloth secured by a leather belt. Both for warmth and protection in the woods, men sometimes wore separate leggings that extended to the top of the thighs and were suspended from the belt. In this illustration, which shows a summer scene, the man's breechcloth is not visible below the edge of his trade shirt, and the weather is too warm for leggings, but illustrations in Part 3 show both of these garments. Women wore knee-length skirts and leggings and may also have worn breech cloths under the skirts (Haviland and Power, 167; Wilbur, 83). The traditional deerskin or moose hide shirts worn by both men and women were sometimes beautifully decorated on the borders. They were sleeveless, but separate sleeves could be tied on across the body under the shirts in colder weather (Brink; Haviland and Power, 165). By the late eighteenth century, heavy woolen cloth was widely available as a substitute for leather in garments, and trade shirts were often worn. Fur robes provided winter warmth and both men and women wore moccasins and a variety of traditional hats, headdresses, and hair decorations.

When the Abenaki adopted certain of the settlers' garments, such as the men's shirt and the women's shift, they wore this clothing as the functional equivalent of their traditional skin garments, that is, as outer wear rather than as underwear (Day). The new settlers in the northern forests and river valleys also came to know and to use certain items of Abenaki clothing and materials (notably moccasins, leather leggings, and the use of deerskin for some European-style clothing) when these adaptations made sense for their daily lives.

A Word About Children's Clothing

Until the mid-eighteenth century, European and colonial children had been dressed as miniature adults, in the same constricting clothing, including corsets. The notion of a child as a developing being, entitled to freedom from physical restraint, entered into English and French thought through the writings of John Locke (Some Thoughts on Education (1693), discussed at length in Samuel Richardson's novel Pamela (1740)) and Jean-Jacques Rousseau (Émile (1762)). By the 1780s, the effect of these ideas was to give children more comfortable clothing: loose trousers for boys, based on the clothing of sailors and laborers, and sashed loose dresses for girls (Buck, [Dress] 204-06). These children's styles foreshadowed changes that were to occur some twenty years later in adult clothing (Baumgarten, 76-78).

Children of both sexes wore dresses or petticoats until they were about five years old, when boys were put into trousers. These trousers had a "fall" or flap front, as did men's breeches, and were either loose at the legs or tied around the ankle. The transition to distinctively boys' clothing made a great impression on John Neal of Portland, Maine, who had a twin sister. He recollected that, around 1798, "they put me into jacket-and-trousers; whereupon, they say that I gathered up my petticoats and flung them to my sister, saying, 'Sis may have these: they're too good for me.' . . . [W]e had always been dressed alike, . . . but from that time forward, I was the man-child and she — poor thing! only 'Sissy,' and obliged to wear petticoats" (Mussey, 23).

Unlike men's shirts, boys' shirts were made to be worn open at the neck, and the collar was shaped to spread out on top of the lapels of the jacket (Baumgarten, 77; Peale, C., painting: The Stoddard Children). The jacket and trousers were sometimes worn with a sash at the waist, but as waistlines in general grew shorter, trousers were made to button onto the jacket. This was called a "skeleton" suit and was the accepted dress for young boys well into the nineteenth century. These suits were commonly made of rough linen tow cloth or of fustian, a coarse twill woven of mixed linen and cotton (Tyler, 154).

Little boys and girls wore dresses made in basically the same manner as the muslin "chemise" gown was later made for women. The little boy feeding the chickens is wearing one in the illustration for Clothing in the New Settlements. When Sarah Emery was about four years old, in 1791, she was allowed to go to Sunday meeting, and her grandmother's "famously embroidered linen cambric christening frock" was remodeled for her Sunday dress, which she wore with a green silk bonnet and a pair of red shoes made by her grandfather (Emery, 15). These dresses were made with drawstrings at the waist, mid-chest, and neckline, and often had a drawstring mid-sleeve as well as at the edge of the elbow-length or shorter sleeve. No neckerchief was worn with them. Earlier in the century they had been made of printed cotton fabrics (Bradfield, 71), but by the mid-1780s girls' dresses were more commonly made of white muslin, usually tied with a blue or pink satin sash. The adoption of this style by women is discussed in the section on the muslin "chemise" gown.

Part 2

The Individual Garments

Women's Clothing

The Shift
The Stays
The Pockets
The Petticoat and the Skirt
The Gown
  The Open and the Round Gown
  The Shortgown
  The Muslin Chemise Gown
The Neckerchief
The Apron
Hair and Headgear

Men's Clothing

The Shirt
The Cravat and the Stock
Breeches, Trousers, and the Breechcloth
The Waistcoat
The Coat
The Man's Frock
Hair and Headgear

Men's and Women's Stockings and Leggings

Men's and Women's Shoes and Moccasins

Women's Clothing

In the established towns and new settlements, a woman began dressing by putting on her shift. Over that went the stays or corset and a pair of pockets tied about the waist. Stockings were held up with braided, knitted, or ribbon garters. Beyond that stage, what was put on varied with the work (or lack of it) that the woman expected to face during the day and the time of day or occasion for which the clothing would be worn. (No more would we today wear the same clothing to work in the garden as to go shopping in town, go to a dance, or attend a concert.) For work at home or on the farmstead, a likely combination was a petticoat and shortgown worn with an apron and neckerchief, all of serviceable materials. For visiting town or friends, or attending church or an event such as a dance, wedding, or election celebration, the same woman might have chosen a printed cotton open gown over a petticoat, with the neckline filled in with a muslin kerchief. A more fashionable woman in the larger towns probably wore a gown in the same cut, but made of a paper-thin silk called "lustring" (or lutestring) or an imported cotton chintz or silk satin. Her fifteen-year-old daughter was more likely to wear one of the newer muslin "chemise" gowns with a wide satin sash. Even fairly fashionable people owned only a few gowns, compared with a present-day American wardrobe.

As styles changed, gowns were retrimmed or remodeled rather than discarded when they still could be worn. Women who understood how to cut or remodel a gown were in great demand in towns and rural areas, even if the women of the household would then do the hand sewing needed to put the pieces together (Emery, 47). One of the reasons so few women's gowns survive from this period is that women had them remodeled as waistlines began to rise in the mid-1790s, or saved and remodeled them beginning in the 1830s when the fashion had returned to wide skirts and a defined natural waistline.

The traditionally dressed Abenaki woman wore a knee-length deerskin or trade cloth skirt, and may have worn a breechcloth under the skirt. She wore leggings in the woods and in colder weather. Her traditional upper garment was a soft deerskin (or perhaps moose hide) tunic or mantle.

While the jewelry available to eighteenth-century women is in general beyond the scope of this book, one item of jewelry common in towns and new settlements — a simple necklace of gold beads — appears so often in the portraits and primary sources that it should be mentioned. One source describes it as having been "all but universal" (Goodhue, 139). Judging from both fashionable and folk portraits these necklaces were rather short, although this style might have depended more on how many beads one could afford than on the dictates of fashion (Earl, J., painting: Mrs. William Mills and her daughter; Emery, 13; Hollister, 96; Steele, 12; Unknown artist, painting: Sally Bullard Crosby).

For outerwear both English and American women commonly wore scarlet hooded wool cloaks, called cardinals (Baumgarten, 38; Goodhue, 139; Hollister, 95-96; Sprague, 263; Weeks, 296). The Abenaki used fur mantles for winter warmth (Calloway, 32), and the emigrants to northern New England quickly adopted this use of fur robes, especially when travelling by sledge or sleigh. It seems only reasonable to wear a warm outer garment in New England winters, but for a time shawls were considered more fashionable with the new muslin styles. Massachusetts-born Abigail Adams, writing from Philadelphia in 1799, remarked upon the fashion: "[R]ed cloth cloaks are all the mode, trim'd with white furs. This is much more rational than to wear only a shawl in winter" (Sprigg, 77). Bathsheba Walker of Brookfield, Massachusetts, married William Goldsbury on January 30, 1794, and moved with him to Barre, Vermont, as one of its first settlers. Two fragments of her red wool cardinal have been saved through the years, along with the story that it was she who responded when there was "sickness or sorrow" in the neighborhood, riding out with medical supplies from her home. "Just the appearance of the grey horse topped by Mistress Goldsbury in her scarlet cloak would bring comfort and courage to both the sick and the well" (Fenwick, 3-4).

The Shift

For centuries the linen shift had been the basic European woman's undergarment, worn next to the skin under everything else in the day and slept in at night. Well-to-do women had quite a few shifts; Anna Winslow was given enough linen to make herself ten shifts when she was living with her aunts in Boston in 1772 (Winslow, 47). But while a woman possibly wore one of her shifts to sleep in and another one in the day, garments made specifically for nighttime wear were not used until well into the nineteenth century. A shift was essential to wear under stays, to keep them from chafing the skin. Shifts were worn throughout the nineteenth century, when they were called "chemises" and were more commonly made of cotton by mid-century.

Late eighteenth-century shifts were made from plain woven linen, cut along very simple lines, and sewn together with a stitch that made very flat seams, which were comfortable under the stays (Baumgarten, 16; Burnham, 16; Sprague, 264-65). In the 1790s the shift had a very low neckline (about even with the armpits), which was sometimes controlled with a narrow drawstring in the edge of the neckline. The very long and narrow sleeves of gowns of the 1790s probably required a shift with a plain short sleeve and no gathering at the cap of the sleeve. By comparison, earlier gown sleeves were characteristically elbow length and often had an added set of ruffles attached at the end of the sleeve, while gowns in the early 1800s had puffed cap sleeves which could accommodate a gathered shift sleeve cap.

Shifts are sometimes found with cross-stitched initials, often at the center front neckline, and sometimes also with numbers. The initials enabled a family to tell the different women's shifts apart in the wash, and the numbers allowed a woman to keep an inventory of the family linen and perhaps also to rotate the wearing of the shifts.

Abenaki women traditionally wore a shirt or sleeveless tunic of deerskin, which was made by sewing finely tanned skins together at the shoulders and down the sides, or was made of trade cloth in a similar pattern. Traditionally if sleeves were worn they were separate garments, as the leggings were separate, and were tied on across the body under the tunic. By the late eighteenth century, though, the sleeves were sewn as part of the shirt, as in European types of garments. The tunic could be hip or thigh length and worn with the skirt, or could be knee length and worn instead of the skirt. If an Abenaki woman acquired a linen shift, she wore it as an outer garment, much as the traditional tunic had been worn, belted at the waist to form a serviceable knee-length dress (Day; Haviland and Power, 166; Wilbur, 83).

Making the Shift

The layout diagram shows how efficiently the pieces of a shift could be cut from the fabric as it came off the loom, making good use of the selvages (woven edges of the fabric). The fabric width in the diagram is 30" but a modern 36" wide fabric could also be used full width. Anything wider should be cut to size. Be sure to check the measurements of the person who will wear it, and adjust the pattern accordingly.

Cut out as in the diagram. Note that the head hole is not centered on the shoulder fold; the neckline is deeper in front than in back. Mark the shoulder fold at each outer edge. Sew the extra long triangles to the lower part of the shift with a selvage-to-selvage overcasting stitch. Try on to make sure the neck opening is a good size for the wearer and for the neckline of the gowns that will be worn over it. Narrow hem the neck edge, or hem to form a narrow drawstring casing and insert fine cord or silk ribbon drawstring.

22

Fold one sleeve in half along its length, right sides together, and stitch from the sleeve edge to 4" from the other edge. Leaving the sleeve inside out, fold a gusset diagonally, wrong sides together, and place inside sleeve. Sew one edge of the gusset to each side of the remaining open sleeve seam. Repeat for other sleeve and gusset. Turn sleeve-and-gusset units right side out. Flatten to find shoulder fold of sleeve.

Turn body of shift wrong side out. Fold body over sleeve, matching shoulder folds. Pin armhole seam and sew from top of shoulder to point of gusset on each side. Repeat for other sleeve.

Sew side seams from bottom of gusset to hem. Narrow hem bottom of shift and edges of sleeves.

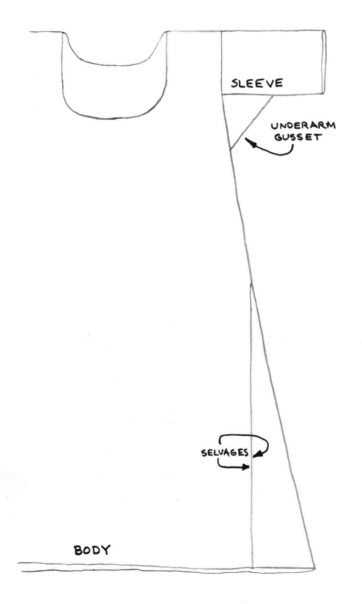

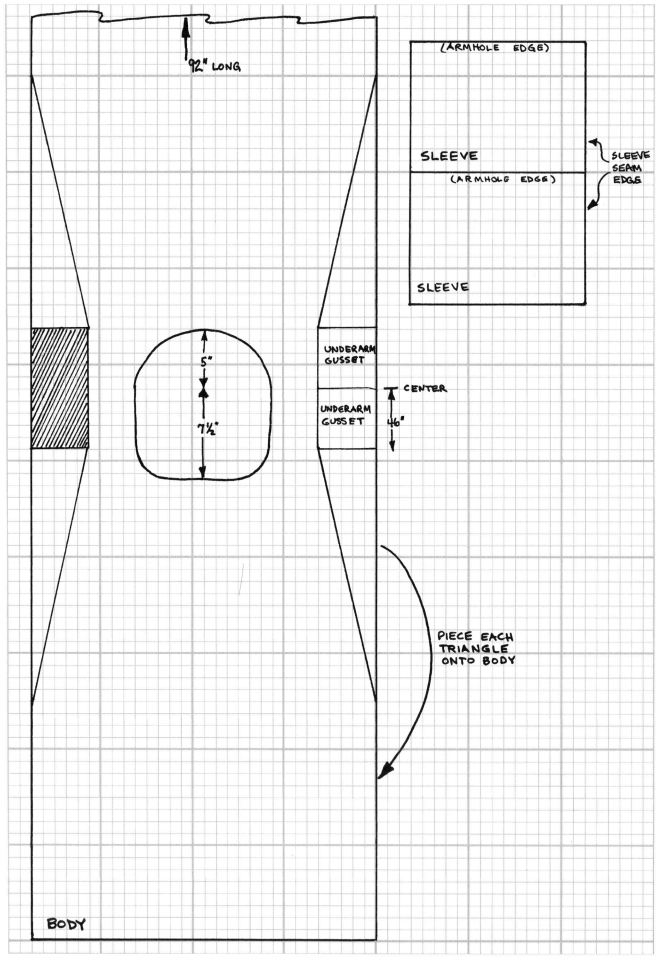

92" LONG

(ARMHOLE EDGE)

SLEEVE

(ARMHOLE EDGE)

SLEEVE SEAM EDGE

SLEEVE

5"

7½"

UNDERARM GUSSET

CENTER

UNDERARM GUSSET

46"

PIECE EACH TRIANGLE ONTO BODY

BODY

The Stays

Just as the shift had other names and other forms in the nineteenth and early twentieth centuries, so the word "stays" was the eighteenth-century English term for what is now called a corset. "Stays" is one of those plural words (like "pants" or "scissors") that originally referred to a plural object: the right and left halves were separate and laced up both the front and the back. (Even earlier these were also known as a pair of "bodies," from which came the term "bodice.") There is some indication that the term "corset" was introduced toward the end of the eighteenth century in France to mean a less stiff substitute for the stays (Waugh [Women's], 77), but at least one writer uses the term "corset" for the one-piece and "stays" for the two-piece garment (Maeder, 179-180).

Stays were made of two layers of sturdy fabric, sewn with neat parallel rows of stitching, which formed pockets to hold in place narrow strips of whalebone for stiffening. ("Whalebone" is not actually bone, but is baleen, the feeding strainers from the krill-feeding whales — the eighteenth century equivalent, along with horn and tortoiseshell, of our plastics.) Stays were sometimes only partially boned, with expanses of canvas in between the occasional bone. The bottom edge of the stays was often cut to form tabs at the waist to enable the stays to spread apart over the hips and continue the correct shape below the waistline (Waugh [Corsets], 44). Unlike mid-nineteenth-century corsets, eighteenth-century stays were not aimed particularly at giving a woman an unnaturally small waistline. Nor were they necessarily laced up very tightly, although there are some contemporary European engravings satirizing fashionable tight-lacing at this period (Baumgarten, 17). The main function of the stays was to make a smooth shape of a woman's upper body -- an inverted cone shape -- with the breasts pushed up to be partially visible above the neckline of the gown. A neckerchief tucked into the neckline provided modesty when it was wanted. A modern woman interested in reproducing the appearance of fashionable dress of the 1790s will not be able to achieve the correct body shape either wearing modern underwear or omitting underwear altogether.

Both earlier in the century and in the 1840s, when gowns had long-waisted, pointed bodices, stays were correspondingly long in the waist. They came well down over the abdomen, and usually had a pocket in the center front for a busk, which was a wooden or ivory board about two inches wide and the length of the front of the stays. The busk kept a woman from bending at the waist, forcing an erect carriage and requiring her to bend at the hips and knees, which was considered more elegant. Busks were often elaborately carved and given as gifts, and they are found in New England museum collections far more often than are the stays for which they were made.

As waistlines rose, first to the natural waist and then above it, the stays conformed to the desired shape, also becoming shorter-waisted, until the extremely flimsy and revealing muslin gowns of the turn of the century required a different shape of undergarment. Also, as the fashionable silhouette promoted more fullness to the back than the petticoats would produce, padding was used to make the back waistline of the gown stand out. This first took the form of a "bum roll," a crescent-shaped stuffed pad tied in place around the waist (Hunnisett, 26; Johnson, 84). But as waistlines rose above the natural waist, small pads or pompons were affixed to the bottom edge of the back of the stays to enable the back of the gown to stand out at the higher waistline.

Probably the best way to think of the stays is as a stiff vest or bodice worn over the shift and under the gown. Whether the stays were worn over the pockets and petticoat or under them may have depended on whether the particular outer gown being worn required the smooth line of the stays to continue below the waist. In fact, earlier in the eighteenth century the gown bodice itself was sometimes boned, making separate stays unnecessary. Occasionally, elaborately decorated stays were worn as a bodice, meant to be seen in the front opening of a gown that was cut to fasten only at the neck and to be pinned open over the stays and petticoat alike.

Although costume historians have documented the use and the manufacture of stays in fashionable clothing of this period and there are examples of eighteenth-century stays in New England collections, they are notably absent from the primary sources. Stays were occasionally mentioned in diaries (Bascom, 22 July 1791), but it is understandable that women did not mention such topics in reminiscences which they knew would be read by others. It is also understandable that the (usually male) compilers of the town histories did not elicit information about such an intimate subject. For whatever reason, the degree to which stays were worn with working clothes remains unclear. It is possible that they were often worn, since women emigrating from southern and eastern New England were used to wearing them.

Making the Stays

The biggest problem in reproducing eighteenth-century stays is what to use as a stiffening material in place of whalebone. Sometimes reeds or strips of wood such as are used to make baskets were used then for stays, but they are not as resilient as whalebone and must be less comfortable to wear. For temporary use, theater groups sometimes use corrugated cardboard (the single-wall kind) because it bends well in one direction but not in the other. One possible material may be the inexpensive roller blinds sold in discount department stores, because the parallel strips of plastic are already sewn together, but they may not be stiff enough. The two patterns given here are adapted from a simplified diagram to use with corrugated cardboard, developed by the Royal Ontario Museum for use with its gown diagrams (see Part 4) and from a pair of stays in the collection of the Vermont Historical Society. Additional pattern diagrams may be found in Hill and Bucknell, Hunnisett, Johnson and Waugh [Corsets].

Whatever material is used for stiffening, the construction technique is the same — the stiffening is sandwiched between two layers of sturdy material, such as canvas or duck. Each pattern piece sandwich must be made separately, and then the completed pieces are sewn together. It is very important to maintain the correct direction of the strips of whalebone-substitute, because that is what determines the ultimate shape of the body in the stays. Cut out two pieces of fabric for each pattern piece, leaving a generous seam allowance in the direction perpendicular to the bones, because some of the length of the fabric will be taken up by stitching between the bones. Starting at one edge, stitch along the seam allowance through both layers of fabric. This creates one edge of the first channel or pocket for the first "bone." Next, put the bone in place, and stitch up next to it. Repeat to the other edge of the pattern piece. A zipper foot or hemming foot will be helpful for machine stitching.

Work the eyelets in the center back pieces in an empty channel between the bones, and put one more bone at the outer edge of the center back pieces for reinforcement.

Sew the pattern pieces together, trim close to the seam, and overcast to finish the seam allowance. Then trim the fabric at the top and bottom edges, and the center back edges, and finish those edges by applying a binding of soft leather or cloth.

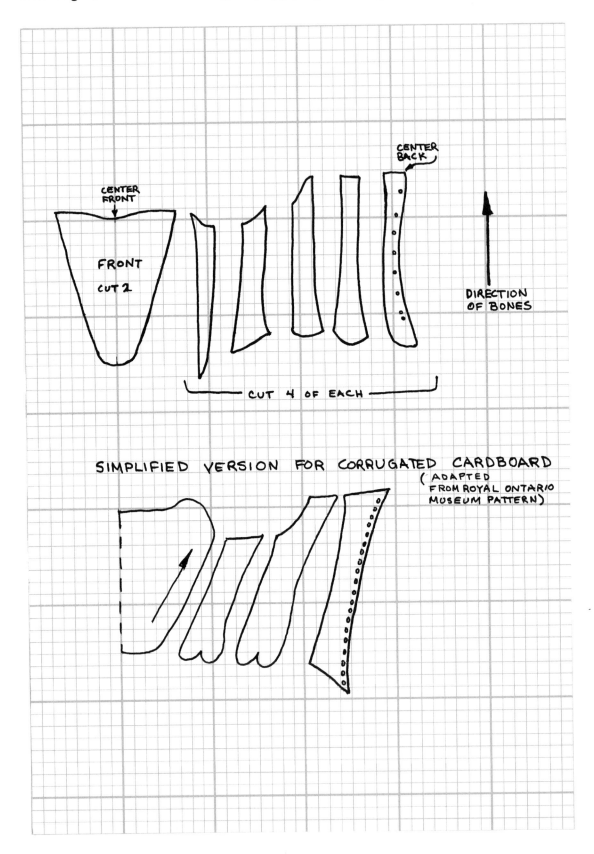

CENTER BACK

CENTER FRONT

FRONT

CUT 2

DIRECTION OF BONES

— CUT 4 OF EACH —

SIMPLIFIED VERSION FOR CORRUGATED CARDBOARD

(ADAPTED FROM ROYAL ONTARIO MUSEUM PATTERN)

The Pockets

When, as a child, I first encountered this old English nursery rhyme, I was very puzzled:

> Lucy Locket lost her pocket,
> Kitty Fisher found it;
> Not a penny was there in it,
> Only ribbon round it.

(It can be sung to the tune of "Yankee Doodle" (Opie, 279).) I wondered how in the world anyone could lose a pocket, since pockets were built into one's clothing, and hard to misplace.

As it turns out, eighteenth-century European and colonial women's clothing did not incorporate pockets, either in the seams of skirts or the way men's coat pockets were attached behind slits in the outer fabric. Instead, throughout the century women wore pockets that were separate objects, attached to a waistband and tied on underneath the petticoat. Petticoats had slits at one or both side seams for access to the pockets.

Usually worn as a pair, pockets look very odd indeed to the modern eye. They are flat and generally pear-shaped, with a slit in the upper portion of the front to reach the contents. A pair of pockets might be utilitarian and plain or made in a patchwork design. Pockets were also suitable objects for decorating with crewel-work embroidery, and often were embroidered by a girl for her trousseau or to give as a gift, since one size fits all (Fennelly [Garb], 32; McClellan, 239; Swan, 112).

After the soft cotton, high-waisted styles with narrower skirts came in around 1800, women's pockets were no longer worn with fashionable clothing. A pocket would have been lumpy and obtrusive under the lightweight and sometimes almost sheer muslin or silk outer fabrics. When women's pockets went out of use their function was served by a "reticule" or small drawstring bag carried in the hand.

The word "pocketbook" did not at that time refer to a woman's hand bag. In the 1790s, a "pocketbook" was what is now called a wallet, carried by a man in his coat pocket, and is discussed in the section on men's coats.

Making the Pockets

Pockets are easy to make and a good project for patchwork or embroidery. If they are to be pieced or embroidered, of course, the patchwork or embroidery should be done before the pocket is cut out.

Cut a waistband to the waist measurement of the wearer and about 2" wide, plus two pieces of 3/4" or 1" wide twill tape long enough to tie in a bow, for the tie ends. The waistband can be pieced together from smaller pieces of fabric. Cut two pieces for each pocket — one front and one back. The back can be made of sturdier material than the front, and is not decorated. Cut the slit as shown in the front piece of each pocket only, and finish the cut edge with seam binding. Place the front on the back, right sides together, and stitch from one top corner all the way around the outside edge to the other top corner, leaving the top edge free. Turn and press. The sewn edge can be top-stitched or further finished with bias binding. Fold the waistband lengthwise with wrong sides together and raw edges turned under 1/4", and press. Insert the top edge of each pocket at the desired place along the waistband and pin.

Sew the waistband edges with overcasting stitch, hemstitching to the pockets on both sides. Sew the twill tape pieces to each end of the waistband.

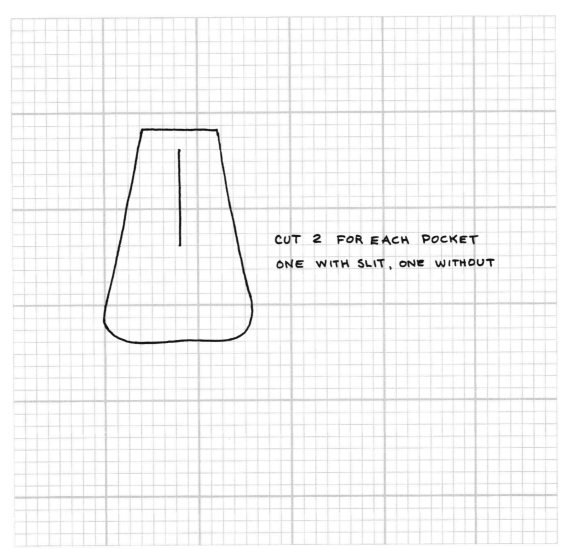

CUT 2 FOR EACH POCKET
ONE WITH SLIT, ONE WITHOUT

The Petticoat and the Skirt

It is helpful to think of the eighteenth century "petticoat" as meaning what is now meant by the term "skirt." Just as a man's shirt was considered underwear in the 1790s but is respectable outerwear today, so a woman's petticoat in the 1790s was considered respectable outerwear — meant to be seen by the public — and not just the slip or undergarment it is considered today.

The petticoat was a piece of clothing of extremely simple construction, with no gores or darts or gussets, made of rectangular pieces of material either pleated onto a waistband or with a casing for a drawstring waistband. Fashionable women wore several layers of petticoats to give their skirts the right shape, and to provide modesty when the outer gown or petticoat was raised for walking or getting into a carriage (Smithsonian, 14). In New England quilted petticoats or several layers of petticoats were useful for warmth in winter.

The outermost petticoat, whether worn with a shortgown or a gown with long skirts open in the front, was definitely meant to be seen. It was made of the same sorts of materials as the gowns: fine silks or printed cottons, or homespun linen or wool (Tyler, 160; Weeks, 296). The petticoat was often made of the very same material as the gown worn over it, but it could also be made from a contrasting fashion fabric. Petticoats of this period were sometimes quilted in an elaborate design of swags or vines, as in the illustration (Fennelly [Garb], 36).

The traditional Abenaki women's skirt was initially made of deerskin or moose hide and constructed as a wraparound garment, with the opening at the right hip and held in place at the waist with a leather belt (Day). Unlike the settlers' petticoats, which were long and worn without underdrawers, the Abenaki skirt was knee length, and several sources suggest it was worn with a breechcloth (Haviland and Power, 167; Wilbur, 83). It was a design well suited to be made from a length of trade cloth, as that blue or red woolen material came into use by the Abenaki. Later the skirt was sewn with a side seam, but it is unclear when the transition from the wraparound to the sewn seam style was made. The Abenaki skirt was worn with a mantle or tunic and often with leggings as well.

Making the Petticoat

The construction of the petticoat is very simple, whether it was worn as an outer garment or under a gown. The pattern pieces are simply rectangles the width of the woven fabric, sewn up the sides and attached to a waistband or finished with a drawstring in a waist casing. If the petticoat is to be quilted, sew together all the required lengths of material but leave one side seam free. Then cut the lining and the batting. To avoid having to hem the petticoat after it is quilted, sew the lining to the outer fabric at what will be the bottom edge of the petticoat, right sides together. Turn and press. Then insert the batting between the layers and do the quilting, and then complete the petticoat. The batting should be omitted in the upper several inches of the petticoat, to allow it to be pleated into the waistband.

Petticoats from this period vary between 85" to 118" circumference at the hem, depending on the width of the woven fabric and how heavy it was. Bulkier fabric is harder to pleat or gather into a waistband, and so should be on the narrower end of this range. To avoid cutting any fabric lengthwise and having to hem a long edge, try to use full widths of the material. Thus, a petticoat may be made of two lengths of 45" wide material (measuring 90" around at the hem, minus seam allowances) or three lengths of 36" wide material (108" around at the hem) or five lengths of 22" material (110").

Measure the desired length for wearer and add 10" to allow for hemming, fitting at the waist, and a drawstring casing if required. If the material is very expensive, fitting in advance with a muslin mock-up may allow this ten-inch allowance to be reduced. (Consult Hunnisett for good instructions on fitting.) Cut the required number of lengths of material.

If a single pocket will be worn, sew up all side seams, leaving one open 8" from the top edge. If two pocket slits are needed, also leave the opposite side seam open 8" from the top edge. Narrowly hem the pocket slits. If desired, they can be reinforced with binding. Note that if an uneven number of lengths of material were used, the second pocket slit will not fall on a seam. The slit must then be cut into the material 8" down from the top edge, and bound all the way around with narrow binding.

In modern dressmaking the hem is the last thing to be done when making a garment. But in order to be sure that the material will hang straight at the hem, when making the petticoat it is better to hem it first and then to make all adjustments at the waist before attaching the waistband. After the petticoat is hemmed, put on all undergarments (including the bum roll if one will be worn) and the appropriate shoes. Put on the petticoat, securing it with a string tied around the waist, and adjusting it so the side seams are at the sides and the material is evenly distributed. Then have a helper pull up on the material at the waist until the hem hangs evenly, and mark the waistline. Take the petticoat off, noting which is the front and which the back, fold under the raw top edge at the marked waistline, and press. If it is not too bulky, the petticoat may be put on a drawstring all the way around. To do this, form a drawstring casing on the wrong side of the waist by cutting the turned under material evenly about 1 1/4" from the waistline, turning under the raw edge 1/4", and hemming the casing to the back of the petticoat, or sewing through the casing edge and the petticoat if the material is very fine. Insert a cord, twill tape, or ribbon to serve as the drawstring.

Quilted petticoats and heavier plain ones, such as woolen ones, should be pleated onto a waistband, which can close with a hook and eye at one of the pocket slits. The pleats are inverse knife pleats about 1" deep and about 2" apart, depending on the size of the person, the width of the petticoat, and the preferences of the person making the petticoat. A typical pattern of pleats is illustrated.

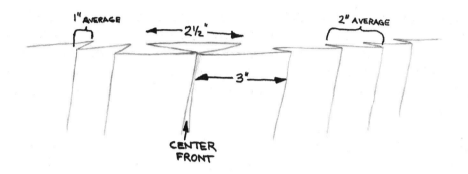

One ingenious waist closure arrangement, which probably provides the best compromise between attractive fit and adjustability, can be done for a petticoat with two pocket slits. In this method the front of the petticoat is pleated onto a front waistband which is slightly less than half the wearer's waistline measurement, and two long pieces of twill tape are sewn to the ends of this waistband. The back of the petticoat is made with a drawstring casing wide enough for two drawstrings to pass inside it. Each twill tape passes through the drawstring casing and out the other end, allowing the back waistline to be gathered comfortably. The twill tape ends are then tied in front and tucked in.

A very lightweight petticoat may be lined, but in any case should be faced at the hem with a 5" or 6" band of medium weight cotton or linen, or lightweight wool.

The Gown

European women's dress of the seventeenth and eighteenth centuries was characterized by some variety of gown, which was worn over stays and a petticoat or hoop framework. High fashion of the time used the French term "robe" to describe various styles, but New England primary sources use the term "gown." (The word "dress," by the way, carried the sense of "what one wears in public" and applied to both men and women.)

One style of mid-eighteenth-century gown, familiar from Watteau's paintings, was somewhat fitted in front but in back was made of panels of material which hung to the floor from the shoulders. This was called a sack-back gown or "robe à la française." A gown whose fullness in the back was fitted by sewn-down pleats (although the fabric was still cut in one length from the neck to the hem in back) was called the "robe à l'anglaise." Sometimes the skirts of the gown were draped up by pulling the edges through the pocket slits, or were looped up by tying ribbons or tapes sewn inside for that purpose. In the late eighteenth century, various kinds of fitted jackets were sometimes worn with matching petticoats. Even fashionable people did not have an entirely new wardrobe made each year to keep up with changing fashions. Instead, gowns were retrimmed or made over — one reason why so few examples of earlier styles have come down to the present time. There were, of course, many more variations than can be covered in this book, even for its narrow time period. For more examples consult Arnold, Boucher, Bradfield, Buck, Hill and Bucknell, Ribeiro, and Waugh, bearing in mind that these sources show English and French rather than American examples.

The national bicentennial made somewhat familiar the styles of 1776. These gowns, whether they had the loose or the fitted back, usually had a rather square neckline, a fitted bodice coming to a point below the natural waistline in front, and elbow-length sleeves with sleeve ruffles. The skirts of the gown were split open to show the petticoat in front and were pleated onto the bodice in front, but the center back sections were cut of one piece of fabric from the neckline to the hem. Gowns of the 1770s were usually made of fabrics with moderate size brocade or printed chintz patterns or from rather stiff and shiny silk satins.

By the mid-1780s, this style had developed into a somewhat simpler and less formal gown, likely to have the fitted type of back and made in lighter fabrics and patterns. Sarah Emery described Newburyport, Massachusetts, women in their Sunday best: "Elderly women in . . . thick silks or bright chintzes. . . .[m]ore youthful matrons and maidens . . . in lighter silks, white muslins, or cambric calicos. . ." (Emery, 16). The neckline was still usually a rounded square, and usually (but not always) filled in for modesty's sake with a fine muslin neckerchief or "buffont." The bodice of the dress fitted smoothly over the stays. The skirts of the gown were more likely to be cut separately and sewn to the bodice at the waistline all the way around. Some museums have examples of gowns of an earlier style that had been cut apart at the waistline and remodeled in the newer style (Miller). The skirts of the gown also did not come as far around to the front, allowing more of the petticoat to show. While no hoops were worn to give volume to the skirt, women often wore a pad or "bum roll" tied at the back of the waist to give more emphasis to the back of the gown.

Young women were also beginning to wear a less structured style of gown made of soft cotton fabric and called a "chemise gown" or simply a "muslin." Worn with a wide sash, this style had developed from the styles of dress reserved for young children in the 1770s and early 1780s. As the century drew to a close, in both the new "chemise" gown type of gown and the older open gown style, the waistline began to rise and the skirts of the gown became narrower, foreshadowing the very fine cotton, high-waisted, columnar gowns known today as the "empire" style, after the Napoleonic era.

Not everyone took up the new styles as soon as they became current, any more than is done today. From contemporary portraits it is apparent that at the same time the grandmother of a family might choose to wear an open gown with a long pointed waistline and elbow-length sleeves, the mother wore a mauve satin round gown with the fashionable longer sleeve and a sash at the slightly raised waistline, and the teen-aged daughter chose a new muslin chemise gown with a sash or a ribbon at the high waistline (Earl, J., painting: Mrs. William Mills and her Daughter; Savage, painting: The Washington Family).

One woman might own clothing in both styles, even in a very limited wardrobe. In 1789, when Mary Palmer was 14, she went as a mother's helper to the family of Elbridge Gerry in New York City. She was struck by the "paucity" of Mrs. Gerry's sisters' wardrobes compared with "the present day" (that is, with 1866 when she was writing her memoirs). Each of the sisters had "one silk dress for parties, one white muslin for afternoons, and one calico for morning dress" (Tyler, 121-122).

Gowns that were worn when working about the house or in the new farming settlements springing up in the far reaches of New England were another story altogether. Sarah Emery recalled that gowns and aprons were normally of blue checked homespun, except "upon some special occasion," when printed cotton gowns were worn (Emery, 7). The petticoat and shortgown combination was the common working clothing for women.

Whether a gown was fashionable or plain, it usually closed in front either by being overlapped and pinned, by being pinned to the stays, or by an edge-to-edge closure. Hooks and eyes were used as one method, as were ribbon ties, and some fashionable clothing was laced down the front through eyelets on either side of the front edge. Sometimes the front of the bodice did not meet except at the neckline, and the opening of the bodice was filled in with a decorative stomacher (Tyler, 122).

The Open and the Round Gown

Whether made of homespun linen for everyday wear on the homestead, or of printed chintz or fine white embroidered cotton imported from India, or of rich silk satin, an open gown in the style of the early 1790s had certain typical characteristics. Unlike earlier styles, the waistline seam extended entirely around the gown, so that the bodice was made separately and then joined to the skirts of the gown. While elbow length sleeves were still worn in 1791 (Emery, 13), the up-to-date style had extremely long fitted sleeves coming to or just below the wrist. There might be a muslin frill at the wrist, but nothing like the cascades of lace elbow ruffles which were popular in the 1770s. Necklines were square, often with rounded corners. The sleeves were sewn to the bodice relatively far toward the back. This construction detail made it necessary to maintain an upright posture with the shoulder blades back, for the gown to fit properly.

The skirts of these gowns were most often open to show the petticoat, and they showed more of the petticoat than did the earlier styles, because the skirts of the gown were attached to the bodice farther toward the back (Bradfield, 70; Tyler, 122). But this is also the period which saw the development of the "round" gown, that is, a gown whose skirts met in front and were sewn together so that the petticoat did not show. Round gowns presented the new design problem of how to put on such a gown over the hips. One solution was to use a drawstring or sash at the front waistline or around the entire waistline, as in the muslin chemise gown. Another solution was to give round gowns a drop front, like the front fall of men's breeches. The front panel of the round gown's skirts was set onto a separate waistband or gathering string, and the side seams' stitching stopped about eight inches below the waist. This allowed the front panel to fall open when the gown was put on, and then to be either fastened at the side seam (Andersen, 242-43; Bradfield, 73-74) or tied around the back of the gown as an apron would be tied (Arnold, 42-43). The front of the bodice extended just enough below the natural waistline to hide the waist edge.

These gowns were made of a wide variety of materials. Compared with gowns earlier in the century, the fabrics tended to be lighter in weight and softer, with more delicate patterns. Fashionable gowns were made of lightweight silks, which were striped, plain, or decorated with a small woven pattern or delicate embroidered flowers. One very popular silk material was called "lustring" (sometimes spelled "lutestring") which was a "light, crisp plain silk with a high luster" (Montgomery, 283). Silk satin was also used, as was "changeable" or "shot" silk, a plain weave with warp and weft of different colors (Arnold, 40; Emery, 30). Lilac and white seem to have been particularly popular colors for the lighter weight lustring, but pink, brown, light slate, taupe, mauve, blue, peach, reddish brown, and green were all in use, as was a red and blue shot silk, which would have appeared either reddish purple or bluish purple depending on how the light struck it. Petticoats were sometimes of a contrasting color, and Mary Palmer Tyler remembered, from her trip to New York City in 1789, a dark sea-green gown, pleated almost all behind, worn looped up over a white lustring petticoat (Tyler, 122). Sometimes a muslin gown was worn with a lustring petticoat (Heath, 698) and sometimes the entire gown was made of very fine white cotton embroidered with small sprigs, also in white (Sprague, 266). Printed cottons, either glazed chintz or unglazed calico, were also worn for fashionable daytime gowns. The material then called "calico" bears little resemblance to most of what is sold as calico today. The background of the fabric was sometimes a light buff, and sometimes a very dark blue or reddish brown, and the designs were most often graceful patterns of vines and flowers (Fennelly [Garb], 18, left; Fennelly [Textiles], 25, right; Montgomery, generally; Tozer and Levitt, 23-25).

Emigrants into northern and inland New England brought with them only a very few silk gowns (Thompson, 76). Calico and "brightly flowered chintz" gowns (Emery, 7 and 40) or wool flannel gowns in winter (Thompson, 75) were worn for Sunday best. When she emigrated to Vermont, Bathsheba Goldsbury brought her printed cotton wedding dress with her from Massachusetts (Fenwick, 3-4), but it soon became possible to purchase the calico to make a gown. Some women obtained the money necessary to make such a purchase by doing work such as spinning for other households. At 50 cents for a week's spinning, a woman would have to put in twelve weeks of work to purchase the six yards of material necessary to make a gown (Churchill, 763). At that price, it would undoubtedly be her "Sunday best" for quite a while. Everyday gowns were made of "linen wrought in the family," usually woven in neat stripes or checks (Churchill, 762; Emery, 7; Thompson, 75).

Making the Open and Round Gown

Bodice: The bodice portion of the gown must be lined, except for the sleeves. Make a full size tissue paper pattern adjusted to the measurements of the wearer, plus ample seam allowances. Use it to cut out the lining material. Baste together and try on to adjust for smooth fit over the appropriate undergarments. Mark the stitching lines, take apart and press. Use the adjusted lining pieces, not the tissue paper pattern, as the pattern to cut out the outer fabric. Baste each separate pattern piece to its own lining piece, more than 3/4" in from the stitching lines.

First, sew the curved back seams. This is done by sandwiching the back piece in between the lining fabric and the outer fabric of the front piece. Trim all seam allowances for that seam to 1/4" (3/8" if the fabric tends to ravel). Turn under the seam allowance of only the front lining along the curved edge, and press. Place the front piece on the work surface with the lining side down. Lifting up the edge of the front piece outer fabric, place the back piece (lining side down) on top of the turned-under front lining so that the seam allowances overlap. Taking care to keep the outer fabric of the front piece free, stitch through all the other layers close to the edge of the turned-under front lining fabric. Press the seam allowances towards the front. Then turn under the outer fabric of the front piece and topstich or hemstitch it neatly over the curved seam.

Next, attach the shoulder piece. It is also sandwiched between the lining and the outer fabric, by the same method.

To adjust the sleeve and avoid any wrinkles, check for fit by pinning the sleeve into the armhole before sewing the sleeve seams. Mark any needed adjustments, unpin, and sew up the sleeve seams. Insert the sleeve into the armhole, pin and baste, starting at the back. Ease the sleeve around the armhole so there are no pleats or gathers, and stitch the armhole seam.

The skirts of the gown are made by pleating toward the center, just like the petticoat. For an open gown, pleat toward the center back. The skirts of an open gown measure approximately 92" to 104" from edge to edge. They should be attached to the bodice from the hipbone around the back to the other hipbone, leaving a gap of about 8" to 10" across the center front. The skirts are attached to the bodice by either of two methods. In the first method insert the top skirt edge between the bodice lining and outer fabric of the bottom edge of the bodice, sewing the skirts first to the bodice lining, and then hemming or topstitching the bodice outer fabric over the seam. In the second method, use the oversewing stitch described in Part 3 to sew the bodice edge to the folded-over top edge of the skirt. For a round gown, make a dropped front panel following the instructions for a petticoat with two pocket slits.

There are two methods for finishing the remaining edges (front edges, neck edge, and the bottom of the front bodice forward of where the skirts are attached). In the first method, trim all seam allowances to 3/8". Turn the seam allowances under (inside the edge) and sew the edge together using either a fine overcasting or a blind stitch. In the second method, cut off the seam allowances of the lining pieces, turn the outer fabric to the inside over the lining, press, and then turn under the raw edge and hem to the lining fabric. Hooks and eyes may be sewn at the front edges for fastening, or the bodice may be pinned to the stays or overlapped slightly and pinned closed.

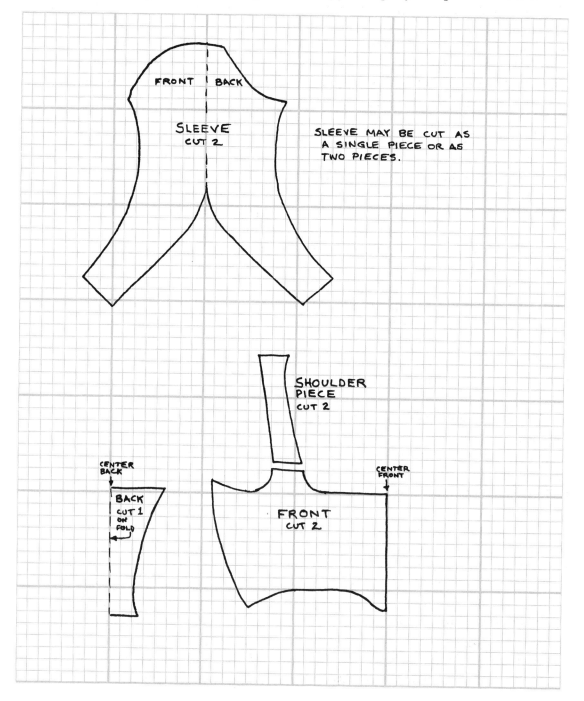

The Shortgown

Although many of the hard-working women in the new settlements and established towns owned gowns, at least of linen or wool flannel if not of calico or chintz, they often wore a hip-length garment called a "shortgown" with a petticoat when at work at home (Tyler, 160; Weeks, 295). Shortgowns are widely mentioned in reminiscences and town histories, one going so far as to assert that "the short-gown at home was universal" (Goodhue, 139).

Despite the word "gown" in its name, the shortgown was not simply a shortened version of the open gown. For one thing, the shortgown's sleeves were cut as part of the pattern piece that formed the body, rather than as separate pattern pieces. Nor did the shortgown have a waist seam — the flared extension of the shortgown over the hips was also cut as part of the body. Quite a few examples of shortgowns are collected in the study of these garments published by Claudia Kidwell. In England and also perhaps in America at this time a knee-length shortened gown called a "bed gown" was worn with a petticoat. It is unclear whether this was a shorter version of the styled gown, with set-in sleeves and a waist seam, or whether this was simply a longer version of the shortgown (Baumgarten, 30-31; Buck [Dress], 114 and 144-48). In any event, this term is not used nor this style mentioned in New England sources, except for one tantalizing mention in Betsey Heath's 1783 diary of "calico short dresses" (Heath, 695).

Today a shortgown would be described as a kimono-cut, long-sleeved, flared, hip-length jacket. The shortgown opened all the way down the front. Some were cut so that the fronts would overlap when they were worn, and were probably pinned closed (Peale, C., engraving: Accident on Lombard Street). Other shortgowns were cut so that the front edges would just meet to tie closed. Enough material to allow for ease of movement was provided by deep pleats in the back which were sewn down to waist level, or by a drawstring at the waistline. As the fashionable waistline rose, the drawstring waistline of this type of shortgown also rose.

The shortgown was worn over, not tucked into, the petticoat, and an apron was tied around it to secure it at the waist. It is possible that the shortgown was sometimes worn without stays, especially if it overlapped in front. Shortgowns were frequently made from indigo-and-white striped linen or linen and wool fabric (Goodrich, 65; Kidwell [Short Gowns], 36), but examples also survive which are made from printed cottons (Kidwell [Short Gowns], 38; Tyler, 160).

Making the Shortgown

The shortgowns shown in the diagram and illustrations obtain their fit with a back pleat, and overlap to be pinned closed in front. Diagrams of other shortgowns with edge closures and drawstring construction may be found in the Kidwell article. The shortgown may be lined, especially if it is made of a lightweight cotton calico, and the lining should be cut to the same pattern as the outer fabric. The lining should be cut first, and used to check the fit of the garment, before cutting out the other fabric.

When shortgowns were made from fabric too narrow to cut the whole garment out as a single piece, the fabric was pieced together.* This piecing was not necessarily symmetrical; sometimes only one sleeve or skirt tip was pieced, or the two sleeves were pieced differently. Piecing was sewn selvage-to-selvage with the oversewing stitch shown in Part 3. Occasionally shortgowns were laid out across the grain of the fabric, to achieve a vertical stripe using a fabric woven with a crosswise stripe.

Cut out the shortgown (or, if lined, the lining), baste it, and try it on inside out over the appropriate undergarments. Pin the front closed, allowing the back material to hang down. Then have an assistant pin the back pleat evenly down the center back to the waist so that the fit is comfortably snug. If two back pleats are desired (Kidwell, 39-40), they should be marked and basted first, because it is difficult to form them evenly by this method. Take the shortgown off by unpinning the front, and make any necessary pattern adjustments, being sure to mark the back pleat line before unpinning it. If only the lining has been cut out, next cut out the outer fabric.

If the shortgown is to be unlined, sew the pleat (which is on the inside), flatten it, and stitch it down through the fabric close to the seam and close to the folded edges. Then fold the front over the back, right sides together, and sew the underarm seams. To avoid shifting along such long seams, pin or baste them before sewing. Start sewing at the sleeve ends and work toward the hem, because irregularities are more easily adjusted at the hem than in the narrow sleeve. Narrowly hem the raw edges.

If the shortgown is to be lined, lay the outer fabric down on the lining, right sides together, and smooth out and pin or baste all the edges, leaving a 6" gap at the center back (through which to turn it right side out). Start at one side of that gap and sew all around all the edges, including the ends of the sleeves, back to the other end of the gap. Reach in through the gap and turn the whole works right side out. Press, and sew up the gap. Then form the pleat or pleats and the underarm seams, as in the unlined shortgown. No hemming will be required with this method.

*Not shown in the cutting diagram.

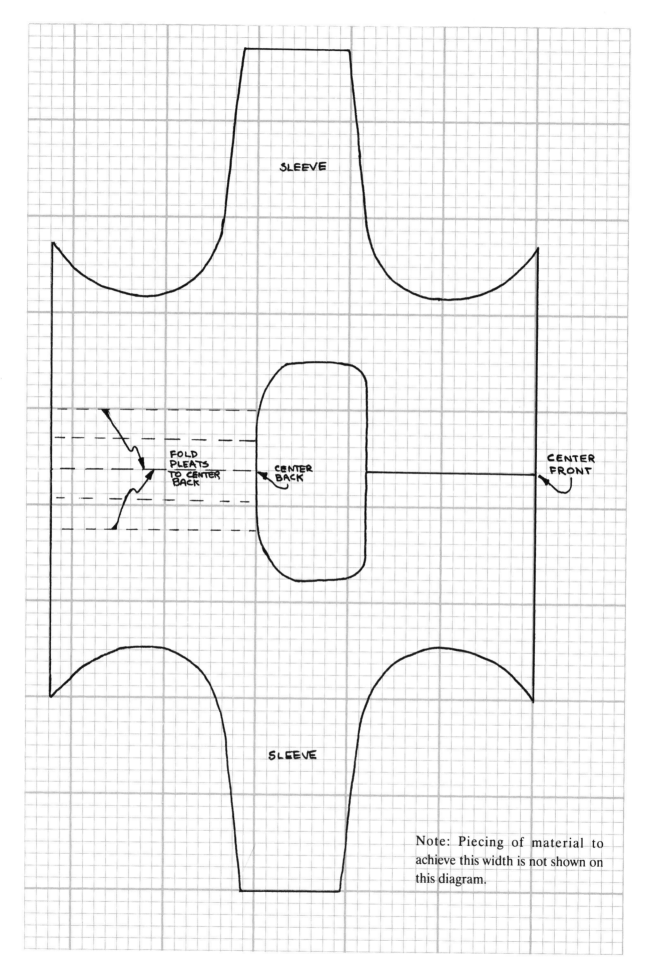

SLEEVE

FOLD
PLEATS
TO CENTER
BACK

CENTER
BACK

CENTER
FRONT

SLEEVE

Note: Piecing of material to achieve this width is not shown on this diagram.

The Muslin Chemise Gown

In the early 1800s fashionable European and American gowns were made of fine white cotton fabrics, sometimes embroidered in white. Emulating Greek statuary, these gowns had the extremely high waistline now referred to as an "empire" style, narrow fitted backs, and their skirts were no longer very full, but were more columnar in shape (Fennelly [Garb], 21; Goodrich, 85; Sprague, 266-67). In the 1790s, a style of gown called a "chemise" gown was popular that foreshadowed this development in fashion. Also made of sheer white cotton, variously called muslin, lawn, or mull, this gown was cut very full, and was given shape by a wide sash at the waist, usually light blue or pink satin (David, [portrait: Levoisier]). The fullness around the neckline was controlled by a drawstring, and another drawstring was sometimes fitted at mid-chest level to avoid a blousy effect (Waugh [Women's], 98 [Diagram XXV]). The sleeve could be short or elbow length, and if elbow length may also have had a drawstring at mid-sleeve to control the shape. The illustration shows an intermediate stage in this development, with the short-waisted fitted back of the later style but the loose front of the chemise gown.

These sorts of loosely fitting cotton dresses had been worn by young girls in the 1760s and 1770s. Another source for this style were the tropical French and English colonies (Boucher, 307), in which the extreme heat made tightly fitting fashionable gowns unbearable. Returning colonists brought the styles back to Paris and London. In 1783 the French painter Elizabeth Vigée Le Brun had exhibited a portrait of Marie Antoinette in this sort of gown (Boucher, 306), which took on the name in France of "Chemise à la reine" and became quite fashionable. Because this style provided so little structure, it had to be worn over stays, although they need not have been heavily boned. At about this period the French seem to have adopted a more lightly boned version of the stays for wear with informal dress (Waugh [Women's], 77).

This style caught on rapidly in the new United States, although the name "chemise gown" does not seem to have been used in contemporary New England. The style is instead referred to as "muslins" or "muslin gowns." Mary Tyler recalled meeting in 1791 an English family which included an "immensely corpulent" mother-in-law, "lately returned from Antigua," who dressed "always in white muslin loose dresses on account of the heat" (Tyler, 168). Although she remarked upon this fashion worn by an adult, by that time girls into their teens generally wore white muslin sashed gowns, and later that year her future husband, Royall Tyler, sent her a present of enough white muslin to make herself such a gown.

Most of the family portraits by this time show at least the girls and young women in these sashed muslins (Stuart, painting: Miss Vick and Her Cousin), even while their mothers and grandmothers were still wearing their silks, satins, and calico or chintz gowns. For a family wedding in 1796, the bride wore a light slate colored silk gown, but eleven-year-old Sarah Anna Smith and her "young aunts" had "new white muslins, cut square in the neck, and short sleeves," with the breadths of the fabric running the whole length from neck to hem, pleated at the back, "and confined at the waist by a ribbon sash" (Emery, 30). Sarah's sash, like her Aunt Hannah's, was blue.

Making the Muslin Chemise Gown

The diagram and instructions are for the earlier loose style of muslin chemise gown with drawstrings. (To make a muslin chemise gown with a fitted back, consider combining the back of the 1809 gown pattern mentioned in Part 4 with the front of the gown shown here.) This early style of muslin chemise gown (Waugh [Women's], 98, Diagram XXV) only requires fitting of the armhole area. Consider fitting this area with a piece of interfacing or spare material, and then add seam allowances and use it as a template for cutting the top edge of the whole gown piece.

The gown as shown on the diagram is 144" around at the hem, but the width does not need to be exact and can vary according to the width of the available material. Use four lengths of 36" wide material, or three lengths of 45" wide material, to piece together to obtain a wide enough piece of fabric for cutting the gown. Fold in half at the center back and, adding seam allowances, cut the top edge to the shape shown. Also remembering seam allowances, cut out the other pieces: two shoulder straps, two sleeves, and one piece 1" wide and 12" long for binding the back neck edge. Ten yards of ribbon or lightweight seam binding will be needed for the drawstring casings, or cut two 4-yard pieces and two 1-yard pieces of 1 1/4" wide fabric for that purpose. Fourteen yards of narrow drawstring cord or silk ribbon will also be needed.

First pin and sew the waistline drawstring casing on what will be the inside of the gown. If a mid-chest drawstring is desired, repeat for the mid-chest drawstring. Insert a four yard piece of thin cord through each drawstring casing. On each side of the center front opening, turn the neckline seam allowance to the inside to form a narrow drawstring casing along the neck edge, from point A to the center front. On each side, insert a two yard piece of thin cord into that casing and sew through it and the casing at point A to secure the end.

Use the stroked gathering stitch (shown in Part 3) to gather the top edge of the back of the gown from point D on one side to point D on the other. Pull the gathers to 9" and pin the end of the gathering thread but do not make a knot or cut it off yet. Try the gown on over the appropriate undergarments, pulling the waist and the chest drawstrings comfortably snug. If the 9" measurement across the back is too narrow, adjust it now. Fasten and cut the gathering thread.

Cut the 1" wide piece of binding material to the correct length, and bind the gathered edge from point D to point D. Sew on the shoulder straps. If a mid-sleeve drawstring is desired, sew the drawstring casing to the outside of the sleeve at that point, being careful to stop short of the seam allowance for the sleeve seam. Sew the sleeve seam on each sleeve. Turn under the bottom edge of each sleeve and sew to form the casing for the sleeve edge drawstring. Keeping right sides together, pin and baste the sleeves into the armholes, with the sleeve seams under the arms. Try on again. If all is well, sew the sleeves into the armholes. Narrowly hem the neckline edge of the shoulder straps. Insert the sleeve drawstrings.

If it is to be an open gown, all that remains is to hem the bottom edge. If it is to be a round (closed) gown, sew up the front edge to the waist, taking care that the waistline drawstring is kept free. Sewing up the front above the waist is optional, because the drawstrings should keep the bodice edges together. If it is sewn, be sure to skip over the drawstrings and keep them free to move in their casings.

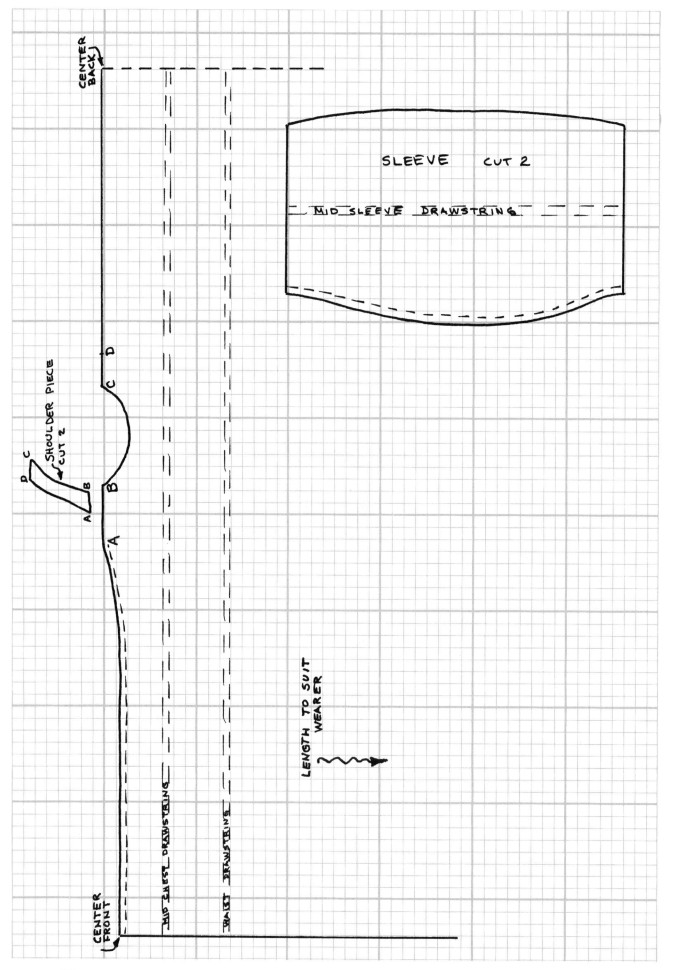

CENTER
BACK

SLEEVE   CUT 2

MID SLEEVE DRAWSTRING

SHOULDER PIECE
CUT 2

D C

C D

C

A B

B

A

LENGTH TO SUIT
WEARER

MID CHEST DRAWSTRING

WAIST DRAWSTRING

CENTER
FRONT

The Neckerchief

Women who wore gowns usually also wore some sort of neckerchief to fill in the very low neckline of the gown. A few portraits of this time show women in gowns worn without a neckerchief, from which it can be seen just how low the gown neckline really was (Gullager, painting: Mathilda Williams; Sherman Limner, painting: Lady in Red). It is hard to tell how much this reflects the style of the portrait painter, however, rather than what the woman would have worn in public.

The neckerchief was a large triangle of fabric, either cut and hemmed to that shape or folded from a square. It was often worn tucked directly into the front neckline of the gown, sometimes with a bow or brooch pinned to the gown at the neckline. The neckerchief could also be overlapped over the gown front and pinned to the gown with a straight pin (Tyler, 160). Sometimes the neckerchief was shaped with ends long enough to be worn crossed over in front and tied in back. The front of the gown bodice also was occasionally made with two straps of the bodice fabric extending across the front, into which the ends of the kerchief could be tucked (Baumgarten, 34, right). Although later sources often use the term "fichu" for this kind of neckerchief, the contemporary sources all refer to it as a kerchief.

The fabric used for the neckerchief varied according to the occasion for which it was worn and the person wearing it. The fashionable neckerchief was usually of very fine white cotton material, sometimes decorated with white embroidery or lace. In the late 1780s and early 1790s, it was worn, in the words of Sarah Emery, "immensely puffed out in front" (Emery, 13). Caricatures of the high fashion of the time show women's faces almost lost behind the enormous kerchiefs or "buffonts." Sometimes a layered effect was achieved with a plain kerchief worn underneath a larger lace or embroidered one tied around in back. Occasionally the second one was made from a sheer black material (Brewster, painting: Mrs. Lucy Eldredge; Earl, R., painting: Mrs. Joseph Wright).

A woman at work wore a checked or striped neckerchief, probably of the same type of linen homespun as her apron (Churchill, 762; Fennelly [Textiles], 16); Merrimack Valley, 88-89). Many of the descriptions of household linen manufacture mention that indigo-dyed checks were woven for aprons and kerchiefs (Churchill, 762).

Making the Neckerchief

Neckerchiefs varied in size from about 36" square to as small as 22" or 23" square. Experiment with a piece of old sheet or tissue paper for the appropriate size. Whether folded from a square or cut to a triangle, the neckerchief should have a simple narrow hem on the cut edges. The selvages (woven edges of the material) need not be hemmed. Neckerchiefs long enough to be tied around the back were sometimes cut out in a pointed boomerang shape to reduce bulk in the tied ends. The curved cut edge has a narrow hem.

Smith, T

Tuesday, December 8, 201

The Apron

Aprons were not only worn by working women in the towns and new settlements, but were also sometimes worn with the fashionable open gown for decorative balance.

Working aprons were usually made of homespun linen, and sometimes of wool, woven in striped, checked, or plaid patterns (Churchill, 762; Emery, 7 and 72; Fennelly [Garb], 35; Thompson, 75). Occasionally they were made of a piece of printed cotton left over from making a gown (Tyler, 160). They were far more easily washed than was the petticoat, especially in the winter when petticoats were woolen and washing (and drying) were difficult operations. As well as serving to protect the front of the petticoat, the working apron also functioned as a handy towel, and could be held to form a bag or sack to help in household tasks (shown in the illustration for Clothing in the New Settlements in Part 1).

The same women who wore aprons of checked linen and cotton for everyday wear also had white cotton lawn or cambric aprons "for holiday use" (Manners and Customs, 227). The author of that essay saw the aprons as necessary because "round gowns had not then come in fashion;" that is, the gowns were open to show the petticoat in front, and needed an apron to cover that opening. Fashionable aprons were made of a very fine white cotton material, which was often decorated with exceedingly fine embroidery in swags or other designs. These aprons were worn as a decorative element with the gown, not to protect it. Some portraits clearly show the details of the fine embroidery on such aprons and their appearance over satin open gowns (Chandler, painting: Mrs. Samuel Chandler; Earl, R., painting: Mrs. Richard Alsop).

Making the Apron

Cut a length of 36" wide material. (If the material is wider, cut it to 37" wide and hem the raw edge with a narrow hem). If the apron material has a lace pattern which should show up flat against the gown, it should be narrower: 22" to 25" wide. The length of the piece should be three inches longer than the desired finished length (30" to 34" for most women) to allow for a hem and a drawstring casing. Turn the top raw edge under 1/4" and press. Turn under again to form a casing or pocket for a drawstring, press and stitch. Hem the bottom edge. Cut a piece of cord or ribbon twice the waist measurement of the wearer, and insert it through the casing. When worn, the apron should be gathered up on the drawstring to about 20" wide. If necessary the drawstring may be stitched to the edge of the apron at both ends of the casing, to maintain the correct degree of gathering, but the apron is easier to launder if it can be removed from the drawstring.

If the material is too heavy to use a drawstring, or the look of a finished waistband is preferred, cut an additional piece of material 4" wide and twice the wearer's waist measurement. This waistband may be pieced together from several shorter pieces of material. Fold it in half lengthwise, with right sides together, and press. Sew from the ends toward the middle, leaving 20" open in the middle. Turn right side out. Gather or pleat the apron to 20" wide, then insert the top edge of the apron in the waistband and sew together with a hemming or overcasting stitch. Hem the bottom edge of the apron.

Hair and Headgear

Hair

(See the illustrations of women throughout this book for examples of a variety of hair styles.)

The 1770s had seen excesses in women's hair styles in England and France and in the colonies as well. Huge towering constructions of women's natural hair were arranged over foundations of wire, horsehair, cow hair, or discarded wig hair, and were then pomaded and powdered. They must have been most unsanitary as well as uncomfortable. Twelve-year-old Anna Winslow, sent from her home in Nova Scotia to spend some time with her fashionable aunts in Boston, complained in 1772 that with her "heddus roll" her hair and cap combined rose higher above her hairline than the measurement from her hairline down to her chin, and that the roll caused her head to "itch, & ach[e], & burn like anything" (Winslow, 71).

Even if rural women did not wear extremely elaborate foundations or powdered hair, their natural hair was worn swept up high on the head. From portraits, the styles seem to have been somewhat wider in the 1780s and more narrow and taller by 1790. In 1787 the New England clergyman Manasseh Cutler described Mrs. Henry Knox, of Thomaston, Maine, as having hair in front "craped" or curled and set "at least a foot high much in the form of a churn bottom upward," with her back hair braided and "confined with a monstrous comb" (Earle [Costume] v. II, 519; Sprague, 276).

In the early 1790s women's fashionable hair styles were still swept back, but were no longer so artificially high. Often the back hair was worn in two long curls or pulled to the front over one shoulder. Large feathers were sometimes worn to complete the coiffure (Emery, 55). By the turn of the century, the fashion for simple muslin gowns in the Greek style called for an equally simple hairstyle that would not overpower the gown. Hair was worn quite short in front and curled about the face, often with a headband or ribbon. The back hair might still be left long, but was caught up in a bunch of curls. The most daring women may have adopted the French style "à la Titus," in which the hair was cut quite short and spiky all around. This is said to have been in imitation of the way prisoners' hair was cut before going to the guillotine, and the effect in France was completed rather gruesomely with a red ribbon tied around the neck and a red shawl (Fennelly [Garb], 8; Severn, 76).

The traditional way the Western Abenaki women wore their hair was in two braids, with some hair at the back of the crown of the head kept out and fashioned into a coil at the crown of the head, perhaps decorated with a small plume, or some shells or beads (Calloway, 33; Day; Haviland and Power, 167).

Headgear

It was by no means universal for women to wear caps, at least about their household business (Manners and Customs, 225). Only the more conservative seem to have

found found caps essential to be worn in public. Cap styles mirrored the popular hairstyles, broader in the 1780s and more elongated in the early 1790s. When Mary Palmer visited her rural aunt and uncle in 1792 she was given lace to make a cap, and soon sported "as high a headdress as anybody." She noted, though, how different her aunt's fashions were from her mother's, who "had then never worn [a cap] since I had grown up, always dressing her own beautiful hair" (Tyler, 160-61). The front ruffle of the cap was carefully pleated and sewn to a band, and a wide satin ribbon often decorated the band, with a flat bow or cockade at the center front or side.

Sarah Emery mentioned the hats which women in Newburyport, Massachusetts, wore on Sundays: elderly women in close black silk bonnets, and the more youthful in silk hats of various hues trimmed with ribbons, flowers and plumes (Emery, 16). Her reminiscences also are a good source for descriptions of the household manufacture of braided straw hats, which became an important cottage industry for New England women in the early nineteenth century (Emery, 60).

In winter, women of the Western Abenaki wore a conical hat made of moose hide or of felt, and decorated with bold designs (Day). Fur hats are described as common among women in the new settlements of northern New England, but the references do not disclose the shape of these hats (Thompson, 77), except that Bathsheba Walker Goldsbury arrived in Vermont wearing what is described from family records as a "handsome stovepipe hat, with two uncurled black ostrich feathers drooping over the brim" (Fenwick, 3-4).

Because some of the fashionable hair styles and caps to cover them were so large, for outdoor wear women often wore a type of hood called a calash, which was a collapsible framework of reed hoops with a fabric covering (most often green silk). It could be pulled up like the top of a carriage over the hair and cap alike (Bradfield, 55-56; Fennelly [Garb], 37; Earle [Costume] v. II, 581; McClellan, 233; Sprague, 276).

Men's Clothing

In the established towns and new settlements, a man began dressing in the morning by putting on his shirt, if it was not already worn for sleeping. Only its collar and the ruffles on its cuffs and neck opening showed when a man was fully dressed. After the shirt, he put on his stockings and his knee-length breeches. Long trousers were not yet in general use, except for sailors and as a sort of overall for traveling (Murray, 29). The long tails of the shirt were tucked into the breeches, and other underwear was not widely used.

To be fully dressed in public, a man wore a suit of clothes, consisting of breeches, a waistcoat (what in America today is called a vest), and a coat. Unlike modern men's suits, the three pieces were not necessarily made of matching cloth. When worn under a waistcoat and suit coat, the shirt collar was closed with a cravat or a neckcloth called a stock. Distinctions between the more and the less fashionable were made by the quality of the materials, the ruffles on the shirt, and the type of neck cloth. The best suits were made of silk or of finely "dressed" or finished wool broadcloth. Men sometimes owned a dressing gown or robe called a "banyan," to wear for comfort at home instead of the closely-fitting coat and waistcoat. The fashionable banyan sometimes had a matching waistcoat (Brooklyn Museum, 20-21) and was made of a silk brocade, while the less fashionable had banyans of linen or wool. For work at home or on the farm, a rougher suit of clothes was worn, of homespun linen or wool, depending on the season. To protect the clothes, and perhaps for warmth in colder weather, men wore a "frock" or overshirt.

Abenaki men traditionally wore the breechcloth, and often wore a pair of leggings as well. Abenaki leggings were suspended from the belt by straps and covered the legs from mid-thigh to ankle, tied just below the knee with a braided or decorated garter. Some version of leggings were also used for winter wear among the new settlers emigrating into northern New England. A loose fitting, soft tanned deerskin or moose hide shirt with separate sleeves tied across the chest and back (Brink, Day), completed the traditional Abenaki men's dress for colder weather, with additional fur robes in deep winter. The front and back flaps of the breechcloth, and the borders and side seams of the shirt and leggings, were often painted with dyes or decorated with dyed quill or moose hair embroidery, or, by the late eighteenth century, with glass bead embroidery.

The Shirt

Like a woman's shift, a man's shirt was an undergarment, worn next to the skin in the daytime and slept in at night. It could be laundered more easily than the outer wool, silk or leather garments. Like the shift, the late eighteenth-century shirt was a garment that was pulled on over the head; it did not open all the way down the front as do modern shirts (Merrimack Valley, 103; Sprague, 260).

Shirts were also much longer than they are today, and much fuller in the sleeves (Baumgarten, 50). They generally reached to the thighs, which is why they are catalogued in some collections as "nightshirts." Other than the Abenaki, who had breechcloths, men of that time did not generally wear anything that corresponds to modern underpants. Drawers made of buckskin or knitted material were just coming into use at the end of the eighteenth century, but these were by no means an essential article of clothing. Because the shirt was long it could be drawn between the legs when being tucked into the breeches, and served for underpants as well as undershirt. It was sometimes referred to, along with the stock or neck cloth, as one's "linen," giving real meaning to the phrase about not washing one's "dirty linen" in public.

The shirt, like the shift, was made from rectangular and some triangular pieces of fabric, cut very economically from the handwoven linen (Burnham, 17; Waugh [Men's], 82). The body of the shirt was made from a single piece of fabric, with a T-shaped slit cut for the neck hole, rather than having separate front and back pieces sewn to a yoke as on modern men's shirts. The collar was fairly high and would fold over if worn without a neckcloth or stock. The neck opening was formed by a slit extending partially down the front, with a narrow hemmed edge. The placket, or overlapping front opening with buttons, was not yet in use for shirts.

Ruffles of a finer linen were sometimes sewn to the cuffs and the front opening. These ruffles showed to fine effect when the waistcoat was put on and buttoned up, and a neckcloth of some sort added. The sleeves were very wide and quite comfortable to wear while working. The fullness was set into the armhole opening, neck opening, and cuff with very fine "stroked" gathering, a technique shown in Part 3 of this book.

Shirts were not always made of the traditional white linen. For everyday hard work, shirts were made of "tow cloth," the rougher linen cloth made using the short fibers left over when flax is combed. Woolen shirts were also worn, and were sometimes made from checked material (Joslin, 77; Weeks, 295).

The traditional Abenaki shirt was made of soft tanned deerskin or moose hide. The skins were sewn at the shoulders and under the arms to form a sleeveless pullover jerkin or jacket with a front opening. The older form of this jacket had separate sleeves, tied on across the body, as the leggings were separate from the breechcloth (Brink; Haviland and Power, 165). By the late eighteenth century the traditional Abenaki shirt had attached sleeves. These shirts were decorated principally around the garment edges. The leather Abenaki shirt, worn as an outer garment rather than as underwear, may have been the model for leather shirts worn by the Vermont forces during the Revolutionary War. When Abenaki men began wearing the linen trade shirt, it was still worn as a tunic with breechcloth and leggings, rather than tucked in, and was often left unbelted (Day). In that respect it was more like the farmer's "frock."

Making the Shirt

The layout diagram shows how efficiently the pieces of a shirt could be cut from the fabric as it came off the loom, making good use of the selvages (woven edges of the fabric). The fabric width in the diagram is 30" and anything wider should be cut to size unless the wearer is quite large. Be sure to check the measurements of the wearer, and adjust the pattern accordingly.

First cut out the pattern pieces and cut the T-shaped neck slit. Narrowly hem the vertical portion of the slit. A reinforcing bit of stitching or patch of fabric may be added at the bottom of the slit to keep the slit from tearing. This patch was sometimes made in the shape of a heart rather than the utilitarian triangle.

Next, prepare the horizontal neck slit by taking fine gathering stitches across the back and on each side of the front slit. About 15" across the shirt will be gathered into about 7 1/2", depending on the wearer. (See Part 3 for instructions on "stroked gathering.") On the back, start 7 1/2" in from the shoulder edge, and sew stroked gathers across the back to the same distance from the other shoulder edge. Pull up the gathers and fasten to a pin, but do not cut or sew a knot yet. Do the same on each side of the front, starting 7 1/2" from the shoulder edge and ending at the front slit edge. Pull up the gathers but do not cut. Then try the body piece of the shirt on the wearer, adjust the gathers to fit, and fasten and cut the gathering threads. Remember that the shoulder seam will be below the natural shoulder.

The trick to making a shirt fit right across the shoulders when it is made without a yoke involves inserting small triangular gussets at each end of the neck slit, before the collar is attached. This gives the necessary width to the neck opening to allow it to sit comfortably on the shoulders. A shirt made with a neck slit but without these gussets will slide backward on the shoulders and will feel quite uncomfortable to wear. To attach the neck gusset in the end of the horizontal neck slit, turn under the edges of the gusset about 1/4", and then fold the gusset diagonally. The folded gusset will encase the neck slit edges. Push the stroked gathers along the gathering thread away from the ends of the neck slit about 1 3/4" on each side, and sew the gusset into the neck slit with an overcasting or hem stitch. Where the gusset is sewn over stroked gathers, take one overcasting stitch into each gather.

Next, prepare the collar by folding it the long way and finishing its shorter edges. Gather the neck edge to the length of the collar. Sew the collar onto the neck edge by encasing the raw neck edge with the folded collar. If desired, sew a narrow strip of material over the neck slit from sleeve edge to collar edge, to further reinforce this area.

Following the instructions for the shift, sew the sleeve seams and attach the underarm gussets to the sleeves, but leave the sleeve seams open 4" above the cuff end. Narrowly hem this opening.

Unlike the shift, the shirt sleeves are gathered at the shoulder before sewing them to the shirt body. Run a gathering stitch from the top edge of the underarm gusset over the shoulder down to the top edge of the gusset in back. Gather until the sleeve measures 11" from gusset edge to gusset edge. Try the sleeve on the wearer and adjust the gathers to fit. Following the instructions for the shift, attach the sleeve assembly to the body of the shirt. Because the sleeve was gathered, to finish the seam on the inside, hem a narrow strip of material over the sleeve seam on the inside.

Following the instructions for the shift, sew the side seams, but end the seams 11" from the bottom. Insert the side seam gussets in the side seams by folding each gusset diagonally and encasing the shirt body edges in the gussets. Narrowly hem the rest of the side seams and the bottom edge of the shirt.

Use stroked gathering to gather the wrist end of the sleeves to the appropriate size for the wearer. Prepare the wrist band and encase the raw gathered sleeve edge in it as was done with the collar. Work a buttonhole in the sleeve band and three in the collar. If desired, top stitch the collar and wrist bands about 3/16" from each edge.

If ruffles are desired, strips of a finer linen material should be prepared and their edges narrowly hemmed before attaching the ruffles. The neck ruffle is 2" wide and 45" long, to be gathered or whipped onto the 24" of the neck slit. Each sleeve ruffle is made in two parts: a ruffle 2 1/2" wide and 30" long gathered onto the edge and up the short ends of the wrist band, and another ruffle 1 1/2" wide and 15" long for the slit edge of the sleeve seam.

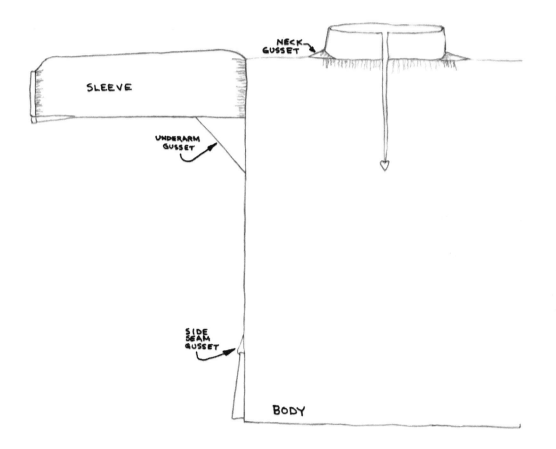

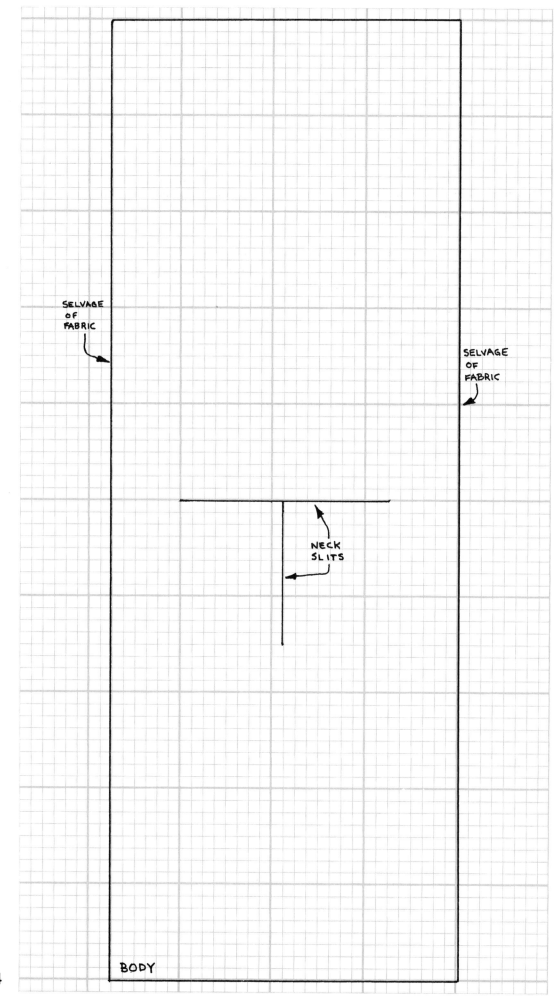

SELVAGE
OF
FABRIC

SELVAGE
OF
FABRIC

NECK
SLITS

BODY

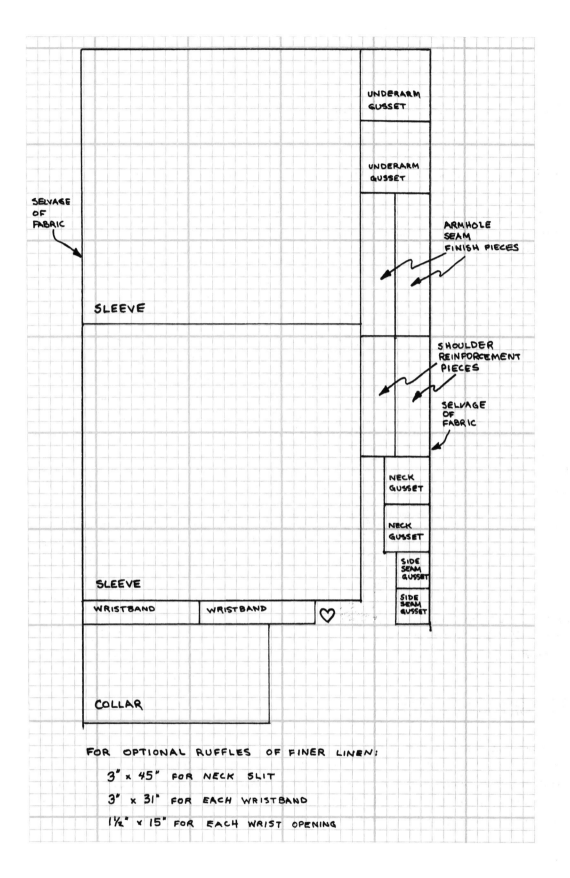

SELVAGE
OF
FABRIC

UNDERARM
GUSSET

UNDERARM
GUSSET

ARMHOLE
SEAM
FINISH PIECES

SLEEVE

SHOULDER
REINFORCEMENT
PIECES

SELVAGE
OF
FABRIC

NECK
GUSSET

NECK
GUSSET

SIDE
SEAM
GUSSET

SIDE
SEAM
GUSSET

SLEEVE

WRISTBAND   WRISTBAND   ♡

COLLAR

FOR OPTIONAL RUFFLES OF FINER LINEN:

3" × 45" FOR NECK SLIT

3" × 31" FOR EACH WRISTBAND

1½" × 15" FOR EACH WRIST OPENING

The Cravat and Stock

Although a man's shirt collar often had buttons and buttonholes, it might be left to fold open while working. But the front slit of the shirt had no button closure. Whether or not the front opening had a built-in ruffle, when it was worn as part of a "suit of clothes," that is, waistcoat, breeches and coat, it would have a very undressed or unfinished appearance without some sort of neck closure.

The neck closure was accomplished with a square linen, cotton or silk neck cloth, folded several times on the diagonal and wrapped around the neck, tied generally in a small bow or secured by a ribbon with the ends of the neck cloth hanging down (Colle, 114). Even when a man was relaxing at home in a banyan rather than a coat, he might still have the neck of his shirt done up with a cravat (Peale, C., painting: Benjamin Rush).

When the neck cloth was pre-pleated or gathered onto a band, and provided with a buckle to attach it in back, it was called a stock (Klinger [Sketch], 4; Waugh [Men's], 82). The stock might show only the pleated band of cloth, or might have an attached bow at the front, just as a cravat would appear when tied.

Rather than going entirely without a neck cloth, working men often loosely knotted a checked, plaid or colored kerchief about the collar of the shirt, even if the shirt collar was left open (Fennelly [Garb], 29; Peale, C., painting: Exhuming the Mastodon).

Making the Cravat

Take a square piece of material and fold several times on the diagonal to form a long strip. Wrap entirely around the neck and bring the ends around again to the front to tie in a small knot or bow. Experiment with tissue paper or pieces of spare material to find the correct size. A cravat requires a square about 30" on a side, while for an informal loosely knotted neck kerchief, a 24" square should be sufficient.

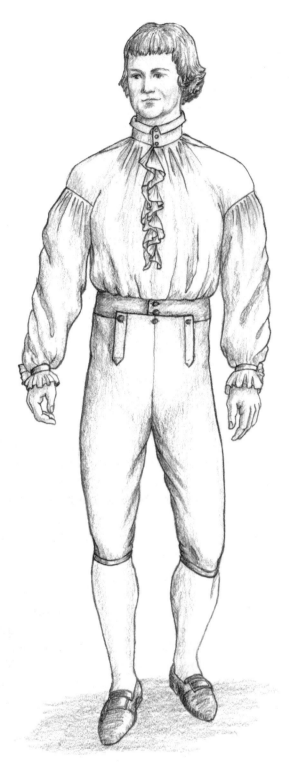

Breeches, Trousers, and the Breechcloth

Some form of knee-length breeches had been worn in European dress since the mid-1600s. In the 1760s and 1770s, breeches had been fairly full in the legs and the seat, and could be tightened at the back of the waistband with laces or a buckle to make the waistband tight enough to rest on the hips. The thigh-length waistcoats and coats concealed the waistline of the breeches from view. By the 1790s, the fashionable waistcoat had a natural waistline and was cut straight across, requiring the breeches to have a higher waistline to avoid a gap of shirt showing between the breeches and waistcoat. Because they no longer rested on the hips, breeches in the 1790s were secured by suspenders rather than by tightening the waistband. (Brooklyn Museum, 17 [3]; Smithsonian, 8). Eighteenth-century breeches are sometimes improperly referred to as "knickers" (short for "knickerbockers"), which is a term from the 1860s and refers to the loosely fitting trousers gathered into a knee band that are still associated with sportswear from the early years of this century.

By the 1790s, fashionable breeches were cut to fit quite snugly in the front of the thighs. To allow enough fabric for a man to move, sit down, dance, or ride a horse comfortably, the seat of the breeches was cut much fuller than would be normal for trousers today. The extra room in the seat of the breeches was also important for tucking in the long shirt. The undoubtedly baggy appearance of the seat of eighteenth-century breeches was also concealed to some extent by the coat. If breeches are made that fit snugly in the front of the thighs but leave out the excess room in the seat as "too baggy" for modern taste, the result is a very uncomfortable piece of clothing.

Around 1800 closely fitting breeches developed into a longer style called pantaloons, which extended further down the legs and were often worn tucked into rather high-topped boots. Pantaloons were very fitted, so much so that they were sometimes made from knitted fabrics, and buttoned down the calf (Brooklyn Museum, 11 [#7]; Murray, 23-26; Waugh [Men's], 81). Trousers, with looser legs and no knee band, were known in the 1780s as sailors' or laborers' clothing (Churchill, 762; Joslin, 77; "Manners and Customs," 226; Tyler, 247; Weeks, 295). Sometimes farmers or teamsters wore trousers as overalls over their breeches. Breeches were far more common, however, even among the new settlers.

Neither breeches nor trousers closed with a fly front. A vertical front opening was used in the early 1700's (Bryant, 28), but was not reintroduced until the nineteenth century, when it was initially considered rather risqué. Instead, the front opening was formed by a flap or "fall" of cloth which buttoned to the waistband with three buttons across the front. This method is still used for Navy trousers, and the Amish prefer this style as well because it avoids using zippers. The flap or fall became quite narrow in the early nineteenth century (Brooklyn Museum, 11 [#7]; Bryant, 30), but the common closure in New England in the 1790s was a medium width.

Fashionable breeches were made of fine wool broadcloth or silk satin, perhaps with a woven-in stripe. They fastened at the knee with decorative buckles. The breeches sometimes matched the coat or waistcoat, but contrasting white breeches were also popular (Emery, 13; Heath, 698). In the new settlements, breeches were made from linen or tow cloth in the summer (Merrimack Valley, 101), and wool in the winter. For ordinary wear this was "undressed" wool - that is, not fulled to make it tighter and thicker or sheared for a smoother finish. It was either dyed with butternut bark or indigo, or was a mixed white and black (or blue-dyed) wool. For extra warmth this cloth could be double woven (Churchill, 762). There are also a few examples of leather breeches (Brooklyn Museum, 11 [#4], Goodhue, 139), which were common at this period in Scandinavia (Grølsted, 18). Even in the newest settlements, a man would have, if he could, a "best" suit of clothes. Such a suit might

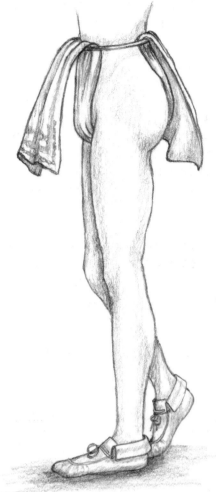

have been made initially for his wedding and could last him all his life, if he only wore it for Sundays, weddings, funerals, and celebrations such as Thanksgiving, the Fourth of July, or election days (Thompson, 77).

The essential traditional Abenaki garment was the breechcloth, which was a long rectangular piece of soft tanned deerskin or trade cloth, worn with a plain or braided leather belt (Haviland and Power, 164; Wilbur, 79). The breechcloth was worn so that a flap of the material hung to mid-thigh in back. The material was drawn over the belt, forward between the legs, and again up over the belt in front, allowing the other end to hang down as a front flap. The two flaps often were elaborately decorated with bead-work, dyed quill work, or other decorative forms (Day). A man's legs were protected, when necessary, by separate leggings, discussed in a later section. In the 1780s and 1790s, in the "Western" frontier settlements in Ohio and Kentucky, frontier militiamen sometimes wore a breechcloth and leggings instead of breeches (Shine, 41), but New England sources make no reference to any adoption of the breechcloth by the settlers.

Making the Breeches

Make a full size tissue paper pattern adjusted to the measurements of the wearer, plus seam allowances. Cut the pattern out of inexpensive material to fit it to the wearer. In other garments this fabric is used for lining, but I have not seen breeches lined other than in the waistband. Baste together and try on over the appropriate undergarments. Adjust to fit, mark the stitching lines, take apart and press. Use the adjusted fabric pattern pieces, not the tissue paper pattern, as the pattern to cut out the outer fabric.

Prepare the breeches front by placing the two breeches front pieces right sides together and stitching the center front seam. Next, cut open the two flap slits. Sew the under flap pieces to the outer edge of each slit, with as narrow a seam as possible. Using either of the edge finishing methods shown in the gown bodice instructions, sew the flap facing to the flap and add the optional flap edge extensions, if desired. Turn the knee opening extension to the inside, press, and hem the top and long edges down to the inside. Work buttonholes in the front flap and in the front knee openings.

Prepare the breeches back pieces by folding the knee opening extension in half to the right side, stitching over the short top edge, and turning right sides out. Press, and hem the long edge down on the inside. Stitch the center back seam, leaving open the top 2". Narrow hem the seam allowances of the top 2". Stitch the inside leg seams. Stitch the outside leg seams down as far as the top of the knee extensions.

Sew each waistband section to its corresponding lining on the top edge and both ends, leaving open the bottom edge. This may be done either by placing wrong sides together and using an edge finishing method, or by placing right sides together, stitching, turning right sides out, and pressing. Gather the upper edge of each side of the breeches back, but do not cut or fasten the gathering thread. Pin the waistband sections over the raw upper edge of the breeches, beginning at the center front, so that the front edges of the waistband extend 1" beyond the center front on each side. Adjust the gathers to fit, and stitch the waistband to the breeches. Work buttonholes in the right front edge of the waistband.

Depending on the thickness of the fabric, each knee band may be cut in two sections like the waistband, or in one double width piece like the shirt wristband or collar. Attach by encasing the raw edge of the breeches in between the layers of the knee band. Sew buttons to the back knee openings. The knee band may be fastened with an additional button and buttonhole, or with a buckle.

Work eyelets the back ends of both waistband sections. Sew buttons on the left front waistband and under the front flap.

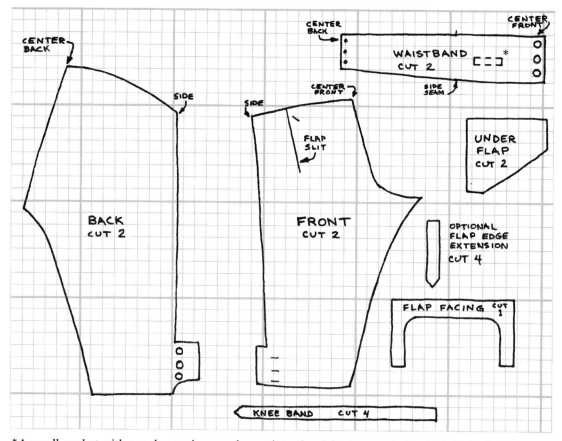

*A small pocket with a welt opening may be set into the right front waistband, if desired. Make the pocket 3 3/4" wide and 5" deep with a 3/4" welt.

The Waistcoat

The second essential part of a suit of clothes was the waistcoat. Earlier in the eighteenth century the waistcoat had been thigh length and served somewhat the same function for a man as the stays did for a woman, encouraging upright posture and preventing bending at the waist. During the Revolutionary War, the waistcoat was hip length. It buttoned straight down the front to just below the waist and continued with flaps cut diagonally back to the bottom of the waistcoat. By the 1790s, however, the fashionable waistcoat style had a natural waistline and was cut straight across, or with just vestigial points. It undoubtedly provided greater comfort and flexibility than did the earlier styles. However, both waistcoats and suit coats were cut with the armholes set farther back than in modern clothing. This required the wearer to keep a more upright posture, with the shoulders held back, so that the clothing would fit comfortably.

Because shirts were thought of as underwear the waistcoat was essential to appearing fully dressed. Often, the waistcoat was worn unbuttoned at the top, allowing the flaps or lapels to fold open, showing the fine shirt ruffle. Even during hard physical work, when coats might well be left behind, waistcoats were usually worn. The waistcoat was not even abandoned when a man wore a frock as a protective working garment (Emery, 190; Krimmell, painting: Village Tavern).

While the waistcoat might be made of the same cloth as the rest of the suit, there was a good deal more leeway for the expression of personal taste with the waistcoat than with the other elements of a man's suit of clothes. Waistcoats were often made of striped (horizontally, vertically, or even diagonally) or patterned materials (Brooklyn Museum, 25 [#7]; Fennelly [Textiles], 20). Fashionable waistcoats sometimes had elaborate embroidery, even when the breeches and coat were plain (Brooklyn Museum, 14 [#8 and 9]; Sprague, 259; Unknown artist, painting: Timothy Swan). Sarah Emery recalled young men on their way to a party in 1791, dressed in "blue coats with brass buttons, buff vests, and satin breeches" (Emery, 13). The same year Betsey Heath noted in her diary that the young men wore striped waistcoats with white breeches (Heath, 698). Sometimes, the waistcoat and coat were made of the same fabric, with contrasting breeches.

Making the Waistcoat

Make a full size tissue paper pattern adjusted to the measurements of the wearer, plus seam allowances. Use it to cut out the lining material. Baste together and try on over the appropriate undergarments. Adjust to fit, mark the stitching lines, take apart and press. Use the adjusted lining pieces, not the tissue paper pattern, as the pattern to cut out the outer fabric. If the waistcoat will be worn with its flaps or lapels open, cut an additional partial lining out of the outer fabric to cover the lapel area, following the dotted line in the diagram. If a welt pocket is desired, follow the directions in any modern tailoring book for making one. The pocket is made in the outer fabric piece before the pieces are sewn together.

One method of sewing the body of the waistcoat is to work piece by piece. First, baste each separate pattern piece to its own lining piece, wrong sides together, more than 3/4" in from the stitching lines. Next, place the back sections right sides together, and sew the center back seam, sewing just the outer fabric together. Turn the piece over, and overlap the center back seam allowances of one lining piece over the other. Turn under the other lining seam allowance, and hem stitch down to finish the center back. Repeat this method for the side seams and shoulder seams, leaving the side seams open about 1 1/2" from the bottom. If a partial lapel lining was used, turn under its raw edge and hem down to the lining. Next, finish the edges (except for where the collar will attach) by turning the seam allowances of the lining and the outer fabric toward each other and stitching through all four layers.

Another method for sewing the body is to sew the back and side seams of the lining first, again leaving the side seam open about 1 1/2". Next do the same to the outer fabric. Press. Then place the whole outer fabric on the lining, right sides together, and baste. Sew from one side of where the collar will be attached, all the way down the front, across the bottom, up and down the notches at the side seams, and up the other front edge, ending at the other side of where the collar will be attached. Turn right side out, and press. Sew the shoulder seam as in the first method, and finish the armhole edges as in the first method.

All that remains is to attach the collar. Place the two collar pieces right side together, sew around the ends and along the top edge, turn and press. Insert the collar in the pocket left open at the neck edge between the outer fabric and the lining, turn under the seam allowances of the lining and the outer fabric, and stitch through all layers.

Mark and work buttonholes and attach buttons as desired.

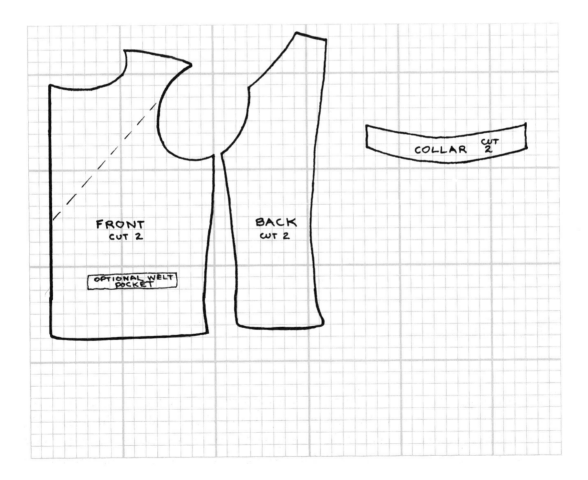

The Coat

The remaining element of the suit of clothes was the suit coat, or simply the "coat." The close fit of the coat back was achieved with curved seams above the waist. The skirts of the coat had pleats at the side seams and a vent at the center back, to allow for freedom of movement. Earlier in the eighteenth century the fronts of the coats had buttoned to hip level and had fairly full front panels with capacious pockets. During the Revolution, the fronts of the coats still buttoned to waist level, but below the waist the coat began to curve away toward the back. The men's coat characteristic of the 1790s had a high fold-over collar and long narrow sleeves, and the front edge began to curve toward the back at mid-chest level. Although the coat often had a row of very large flat buttons down the right front edge and might have buttonholes down the other edge, the buttonholes often were not functional and had begun to disappear by this time. Without functional buttonholes, these coats fastened edge-to-edge at mid-chest level with two or three hooks and eyes.

The large pockets, which were in the fronts of the earlier coats, migrated around toward the sides and back as the garment piece holding the pocket was cut toward the back in a more pronounced curve. In the 1790s coat pockets were still accessible through a pocket flap on the outside of the coat. With the high-waisted styles of the 1800s, the coat was cut sharply away horizontally at waist level in front, and had tails only in back (Brooklyn Museum, 12 [#6]; Waugh [Men's], 80). Vestiges of that style remain in today's formal wear tailcoats, with pockets set into the tails of the coat at the waist seam.

The finest suits were made of imported silk (perhaps a changeable plain weave or a woven-in satin stripe) or fine wool broadcloth. English and French formal suits were often embroidered with elaborate floral designs (Baumgarten, 56; Brooklyn Museum, 12 [#4] and 13 [#13]). The embroidery was done by professionals, on the flat fabric, in the general shape of the outlines of the garment, so that it would appear on the borders when the garment was made up by the tailor. Even a row of extra sprigs was embroidered to be used for the covered buttons. Such embroidered covered buttons on a plain coat are shown in one portrait (Unknown artist, painting: Timothy Swan), but embroidered coats are relatively rare in New England portraits or documented clothing of this period.

All three pieces of a suit often were made of matching fabric, as were both of George Washington's inaugural suits (McClellan, 328; Tyler, 120). It was also common to have matching breeches and coat with a contrasting striped or figured waistcoat. Sometimes the waistcoat and coat were cut from the same cloth, with contrasting breeches. The blue coat with brass buttons was worn then (Emery, 13) and has been a popular combination ever since. Most men who worked farms had a suit of rough homespun wool for winter, perhaps a woven stripe or mixed color wool called "sheep's grey," and one of homespun linen or fustian (a coarse twilled fabric of linen and cotton) for the summer (Goodrich, 85).

Men carried important papers or paper money in their coat pockets in a "pocket book," which folded in half or in thirds and was often tied closed. These were sometimes made of leather, but often were worked in needlepoint and given as gifts. Examples of such pocket books may be found in many books on the history of American needlework (Baumgarten, 70-71; Brooklyn Museum, 19 [#13]; Fennelly [Garb], 33); Swan, 115-16).

Making the Coat

Make a full size tissue paper pattern adjusted to the measurements of the wearer, plus seam allowances. Use it to cut out the lining material. Baste together and try on over the appropriate undergarments. Adjust to fit, mark the stitching lines, take apart and press. Use the adjusted lining pieces, not the tissue paper pattern, as the pattern to cut out the outer fabric. If real pockets are desired, cut two additional rectangles of lining material for each pocket. If cuffs are desired, cut four each of the front and back cuff pieces.

First, baste the back lining pieces, wrong sides together, to the corresponding back outer fabric pieces, more than 3/4" in from the stitching lines. Next, finish the top and side edges of the vent on both back pieces, following the gown bodice or waistcoat instructions for finishing edges. Then, sew the center back seam from neck edge to waist, following the waistcoat instructions. Overlap the left vent over the right, and top stitch across the top vent edge. Then finish the pleat edges of the back.

If working pockets are desired, slit the coat front outer fabric pieces where the pockets are to go. Place an extra rectangular pocket piece right side down on the right side of the coat front, lining up the top edge of the rectangle and the bottom edge of the pocket slit. Stitch close to that edge. Repeat with the other pocket piece, lining its bottom edge up with the top edge of the pocket slit. Turn both pocket pieces to the inside of the coat front piece so that they both hang down, and press. Sew the two pocket pieces together around their other three edges.

Baste the front lining pieces, wrong sides together, to the corresponding front outer fabric pieces from the neck down to the waist. Stitch the pocket rectangle and the top of the pocket edge down to the coat lining. Smooth the outer fabric over the lining and baste the rest of the piece to the lining.

Finish the pleat edges of the front pieces. Following the gown bodice instructions, sew the curved back seams. Overlap the pleat edges of the front pieces about 1/2" over the pleat edges of the back, and topstitch the length of the pleat edges. Form the pleats at the waist and make a stitch through all layers. A decorative button may be sewn on at this location at both sides of the back.

Following the waistcoat instructions, sew the shoulder seams. Following the gown instructions, attach the sleeves and finish the front edges up to where the collar will be attached. Three hooks and eyes may be attached between the outer fabric and the lining while the front edge is being finished.

Prepare the collar, pocket flaps, and cuffs (if desired) by sewing them right sides together around all edges except the edge that will be attached to the garment. Following the waistcoat instructions, attach the collar. Edge finish the top edge of the pocket flaps and topstitch them in place through the coat front and lining. If cuffs are desired, stitch them to the ends of the sleeves, encasing the raw sleeve edge between the two layers of the cuff. Fold the cuffs up to the outside 1/2" below the seam, for a smoother edge. Hem the bottom edge of the coat by cutting the lining to the desired length, and folding the outer material to the inside over the lining, and hemming down to the lining on the inside. Attach decorative buttons at front edge if desired.

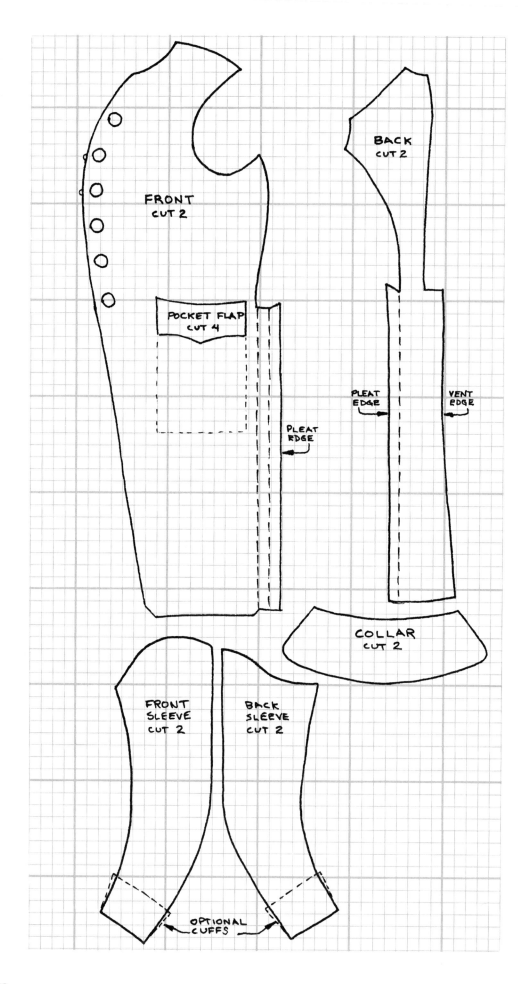

FRONT
CUT 2

BACK
CUT 2

POCKET FLAP
CUT 4

PLEAT
EDGE

PLEAT
EDGE

VENT
EDGE

PLEAT
EDGE

COLLAR
CUT 2

FRONT
SLEEVE
CUT 2

BACK
SLEEVE
CUT 2

OPTIONAL
CUFFS

The Man's Frock

A man's frock was a working garment worn over the shirt, vest and breeches, to keep clothing clean and to provide for warmth in winter. A frock is shown in the illustration for Clothing in the New Settlements in Part 1. In 1799, David Emery was wearing a frock over his "common suit" when he hesitated to accept a dinner invitation, until the "old gentleman . . . in his most peremptory manner ordered David to take off his frock and follow him" (Emery, 190). Although frocks and shirts may have been worn alone for field work in exceptionally hot weather in the South (Baumgarten, 66), this practice is not mentioned in the New England sources. The frock was worn at least by farmers and teamsters (Tyler, 247) in the eastern United States towards the end of the eighteenth century. It was cut like an oversized shirt, with a partial front opening, and was pulled on over the head, but was made of a heavier weight of linen or wool than the shirt.

At this same time, the settlers and military forces on the "Western" frontier of Kentucky and Ohio favored a "hunting shirt" which was made of coarse linen or deerskin, sometimes decorated with fringe. It is described in the recollections of Joseph Dodderidge as a "sort of loose frock, reaching halfway down the thighs, with large sleeves" but opening all the way down the front, and overlapping a foot or more when belted (Shine, 40-41).

In Britain at this time and throughout the nineteenth century, white linen frocks were worn by all sorts of working men (West, painting: The Old George Inn). Nineteenth-century frocks were often decorated with parallel rows of gathering and embroidered, sometimes with emblems of a trade and sometimes with hearts and flowers (Buck [Smock], 17). In the nineteenth century these garments became known as smocks and the technique of embroidered gathers as "smocking." The few frocks shown in American paintings from the late eighteenth or early nineteenth century are also white linen, but do not show any fancy smocking or embroidery (Krimmell, painting: Village Tavern). Lest it be thought that white linen would be impractical for a working garment, bear in mind that although it may show dirt more easily it is also more easily cleaned than are dyed materials. Medical and laboratory clothing in the present day is often made of sturdy white cotton to allow it to be sterilized. Laural Armstrong recalled graphically how, in his boyhood in Dorset, Vermont, in the early 1800s, linen clothing was boiled and beaten in hot lye to clean it (Armstrong, 137-39).

Frocks mentioned in the primary sources were made not only of white linen or tow cloth (Churchill, 762; Weeks, 295), but also of Kersey or coarse woolen cloth (Joslin, 77; Tucker, 110). By far the most frequent description is of indigo-dyed blue or blue-and-white striped linen or woolen homespun material (Fairbanks, 139), and the surviving nineteenth and early twentieth-century examples are blue-and-white striped or checked (Fennelly [Garb], 40). Blue striped or checked frocks were used by farmers in the more isolated areas of New England well into the 1920s, and old farmers in Vermont still refer to their denim work coats kept for use in the barn as their "barn frocks." In the early 1800s Lyman Beecher of Boston annually preached in Peacham, Vermont, in exchange with the Peacham minister. On his return to Boston one year, Dr. Beecher told his Boston congregation that when he had stood up the week before to offer the prayer in Peacham, "half an acre of blue frocks rose up before me, with an honest heart under every one of them!" (Wells, F., 143).

Hair and Headgear

Hair

(See the illustrations of men throughout this book for examples of a variety of hair styles.)

The European fashion of wearing a wig, often powdered white, was as current in the colonies as it was in England or France. The fashion was not immediately discarded after the American Revolution; both the wearing of wigs, and the fashion of dressing and powdering one's natural hair in the same style as a wig, persisted for some years (Emery, 13; McClellan, 328; Weeks, 296).

The first element of the fashion to fall by the wayside was the use of powder, except for the most formal occasions. While some men in the 1790s still wore their long hair bound into a queue or braid and tied with a black ribbon, this style was seen as somewhat old-fashioned (Weeks, 295), and it went out of style by 1800. However, the common styles for men's hair were still long. Although loose long hair for men had been considered the mark of a backwoodsman or farmer in the 1770s, by the late 1780s many portraits show men with what are now called bangs in front, and collar-to shoulder-length hair on the sides and in back.

Fashionable men still curled their hair or wore curled wigs, with a distinct roll or curl worn right above the ears (Copley, painting: Winslow Warren; Stuart, painting: Luke White). The less fashionable left their uncurled hair to stick out over the ears at the same level (Ames, painting: Self-Portrait; Earl, R., painting: Daniel Boardman; Sherman Limner, painting: Man in Red). At the end of the century, the most radical style, taken from France, was to wear the hair quite short and brushed forward from the crown of the head. This style was variously described as looking like a frightened owl, or as if one were walking backward into a hurricane (Severn, 87-88).

Western Abenaki men traditionally also wore their hair long and loose rather than in braids. Young men wore a headband to hold the hair in place, and sometimes decorated the band with one or two feathers. An alternative style for married men was to draw some of the hair up into a coil at the back of the crown of the head and secure it with wooden pins and a leather thong (Day; Haviland and Power, 167).

Headgear

Traditionally, the men of the Western Abenaki had several types of headdress. For winter, there was a pointed hood that came down on the shoulders and sometimes

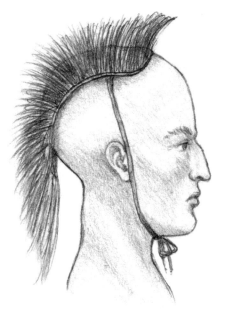

was decorated with a tuft of deer hair at the point. Conical caps of various materials, including birchbark, were also traditionally worn (Calloway, 33; Haviland and Power, 165). One headdress incorporated a pair of deer antlers, while another was a "roach" or crest of red-dyed deer hair, which was tied on the head with thongs (Day; Haviland and Power, 165). The illustration shows this style on a bald head to make clear its shape and method of construction, but it was worn over the natural hair.

European and American men's hats of this time were mostly variations of a wide-brimmed, low-crowned, round felt hat (although straw hats were introduced in the early 1800s (Emery, 61)). If the brim was left round on the sides it was considered to be the farmers' style, and Quaker men, even in the cities, also wore round hats. The brims were at times so broad that they had to be supported by cords at the sides (Goodrich, 85). With the brim turned up or "cocked" at the back and both sides, it is the familiar tricorne, which was worn throughout the century with variations in size and style of the turned-up brims and remained popular in the 1790s (Brooklyn Museum, 7 [#13]; Weeks, 296). The hat was also sometimes turned up only in two places, resulting in the bicorne which is seen in portraits from the Napoleonic era (Brooklyn Museum, 7 [#17]). As the nineteenth century began, men turned to a style of hat with a relatively narrow brim and high crown — the forerunner of the nineteenth century top hat (Thompson, 77; Warwick, Pitz and Wycoff, 218).

Men's and Women's Stockings and Leggings

At the end of the eighteenth century, stockings were much more important to fashionable men than to women, because well-fitting stockings allowed the men to show off the shape of their calves, while on women stockings would not usually be seen, at least, generally not above the ankle.

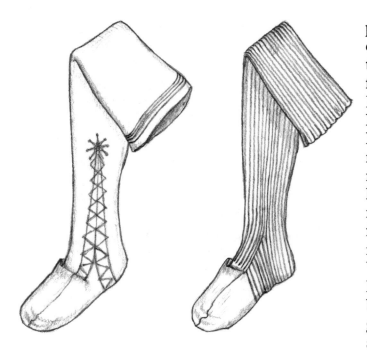

Fashionable men preferred silk stockings because of the fit, and white was the favorite color with fashionable dress (Brooklyn Museum, 17 [#8 and 10]; Emery, 13; Goodrich, 85; Hunter, 145). Garters are mentioned for holding up men's stockings, although the knee bands and buckles of men's breeches sometimes fastened tightly enough to make garters unnecessary. Women's stockings, of course, had to be held up with a braided, knitted, or ribbon garter, which was fastened just above the knee.

If stockings were not made of silk, they were knit of homespun linen for summer (Merrimack Valley, 100) and of wool for winter (Goodrich, 85; Wells, D. and R., 211). Although cotton cloth was imported for women's gowns, cotton thread does not seem to have been as current in New England for knitting stockings as it was in the South. Ruth Henshaw spun cotton thread for her brother's stockings (Bascom, 25 July 1791), but Samuel Goodrich recalled that "[c]otton -- that is, raw cotton -- was then wholly unknown among us at the North, except as a mere curiosity, produced somewhere in the tropics; but whether it grew on a plant, or an animal, was not clearly settled in the public mind" (Goodrich, 71). By the early 1800s, however, cotton thread was commonly used for knitting stockings in New England (Fennelly [Garb], 43; Swan, 24-25).

The knitting of stockings "was performed by the female part of the family in the evening, and especially at tea parties" (Goodrich, 73). Sometimes very fine stockings were made, with elaborate patterns up the outer sides called "clocks" (Baumgarten, 48). Unlike spinning or weaving, knitting was portable, and could be worked on away from home. Some degree of competition for the finest knitting is apparent in Sarah Emery's description of Newburyport's "social tea parties of an afternoon, at which we assembled at an early hour, dressed in our best, with our go-abroad knitting work, usually fine cotton, clocked hose" (Emery, 77).

For everyday use, stockings were most often made of indigo-dyed yarn, or of blue and grey mixed wool. There is some indication that in the South (Baumgarten, 48) and in French North America (Johnson, 121-24) the most poorly-dressed people wore stockings cut on the bias from woven rather than knitted material, but the New England sources do not mention them. Johnson gives instructions for how to measure and make this sewn type of stocking.

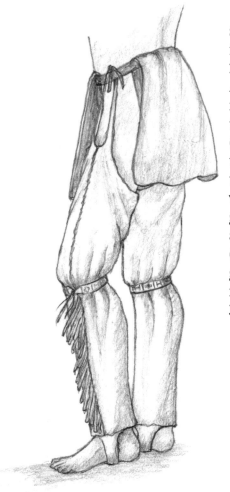

In northern and inland New England, the new settlers sometimes wore heavy woolen leggings for protection against the snow (Wells, D. and R., 212) or wore leather leggings as did their Abenaki neighbors (Goodhue, 139). Abenaki men's leggings came to the hip and were tied to the belt, which also supported the breechcloth (Day; Haviland and Power, 164). These leggings tapered toward the ankle and were decorated on the outside edge of the calf with bead or quill work or with a cut fringe. The leggings were gartered (or "gaitered") just below the knee with a band which was sometimes also decorated (Wilbur, 80). Abenaki women also wore leggings, but women's leggings were knee high rather than suspended from a belt (Calloway, 32).

Men's and Women's Shoes and Moccasins

Although European and colonial shoes were tied with ribbon ties at the beginning of the 1700s, by mid-century shoe buckles were essential and tied shoes were entirely out of style. The rich wore shoe buckles (and knee-buckles on men's breeches) adorned with jewels; those who could not afford jewels made do with "paste" (a hard, brilliant glass imitation jewel) or simple metal buckles (Goodhue, 139; Steele, 60; Weeks, 296). Buckles remained in fashion until the mid-1790s, when shoes tied with strings became acceptable again (Smithsonian, 5-6 and 13-14).

Everyday men's shoes had low heels and came up on the instep in much the same way as today's shoes (Brooklyn Museum, 18 [#12]). Boots were relatively rare until around 1800. When protection from the elements or from high brush was needed, various types of leggings were worn instead (Felt, 140). For dance parties men often wore pumps or slippers that needed neither a buckle nor a tied fastener and were often decorated with a ribbon rosette (Brooklyn Museum, 18 [#16]).

Women's shoes had a graceful curved heel about 1 1/4" high, and were made from fine colored leather or from cloth with a leather sole. John Buckingham's widowed mother was employed in the sewing operations of binding and closing women's cloth shoes in the early 1780s (Mussey, 15). Sarah Emery, whose grandfather made shoes, remembered a red pair he made for her first Sunday meeting, and another special pair of purple kid slippers (Emery, 15 and 35).

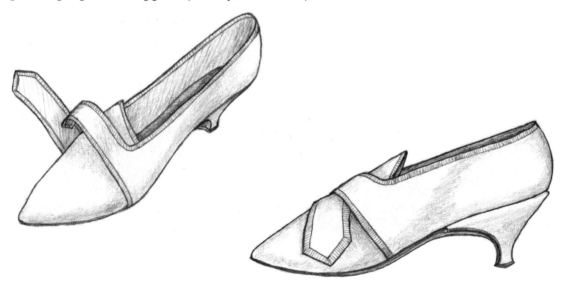

By the 1790s fashionable women's shoes had a sharply pointed toe, and the heel was decreasing in height (Baumgarten, 46-47). In the early 1800s the shape of the

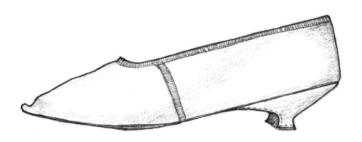

shoe was still elongated, but with a more rounded toe, and the heel had very nearly disappeared. Such fine shoes, of course, were not suitable for walking outside in mud or snow. To solve this problem, earlier in the century fashionable women wore pattens, which were a platform which could be slipped on the shod foot for walking in bad weather (Earle [Costume] v. I, 362-63). Rural New England sources do not mention these inventions, which would probably have been impractical in deep snow or mud. Some sources suggest that people went barefoot at home in summer and brought their shoes to church to put on there, but it is hard to know whether these reports are reliable (Tucker, 111). Children, in any event, went barefoot much of the time, and Amos Churchill recalled that at age 12 he "wore, all winter, the flank of a hide gathered up moccasin-like" and that he did not acquire his first pair of boots until he was twenty, in 1793 (Churchill, 753).

The Western Abenaki moccasin had a fairly high collar and tongue, extending about 3 inches up the ankle. The collar could be worn up or folded down. The moccasin was fastened with a long thong, which passed through holes in the tongue and wrapped around the ankle to be tied in front. The sole of one style (the "beaver tail") was drawn up around the foot and sewn to a vamp piece and the ankle collar.

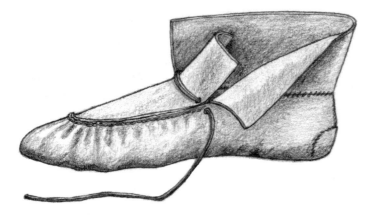

It was shaped at the heel by a seam at the back. The "rabbit nose" design was shaped at the toe as well, with a T-shaped seam, giving a better fit (Brink; Day). For better traction on snowshoes in the winter, moccasins were sometimes made with the hair left on the outside (Brink). An earlier style of Algonkian moccasin was made of a single piece of leather, cut and shaped with a seam up the front and at the heel (Wilbur, 81). This earlier shape may explain why the French Jesuit missionary, Father Sebastian Rasles, in his 1720 journal of his life among the Abenaki, described moccasins as "socks made of elk-skin, and lined inside with hair or with wool" (Calloway, 32-33). Moccasins and snowshoes were widely adopted by the new settlers, both men and women, as more suited to their needs than the shoes they had brought from the southern New England towns (Goodhue, 139).

Part 3

Fabrics and Hand-Sewing Techniques

What Materials Were Used, and Choosing Materials for Making Reproductions

From the vantage point of 1990, looking at real leather and the natural fiber fabrics of cotton, linen, wool, and silk, there is no question that silk, linen, and leather are considered the more expensive and luxurious materials for clothing. Fine woolens come next, and cotton is the workhorse of the natural fibers, suitable for blue jeans and sportswear. In the 1790s, however, even in the inhospitable climate of Vermont the reliable home-produced materials were linen and wool. Leather was, of course, widely available, and tanneries were well-established. The traditional Abenaki methods for tanning deer and moose hides resulted in fine, white hides especially soft and pliable for clothing use. Commercially dyed and finished wool cloth was used for better clothing, while silk and cotton (still largely imported) were considered the luxurious materials.

Cotton: Bathsheba Walker Goldsbury's wedding dress was made in Massachusetts in 1794, and came to Vermont with her shortly thereafter. It is a fine ecru cotton, blockprinted with a design of brown vines and leaves with feathery red flowers. It would have been called a "calico" in eighteenth-century America, from the city of Calcutta in India, and bears little resemblance to the small, often floral, repetitive "country" style prints called calicos today. As well as the fine block-printed stylized designs of vines and flowers, other fine cotton fabrics were imported from India: soft plain-woven muslin, lawn, or mull, sometimes with hand-embroidered white sprigs worked into the fabric. Printed cottons were also manufactured in England (Tozer and Levitt, 23-25), but the American cotton weaving and printing industries were just getting started. A sturdy yellow cotton cloth called nankeen, originally from China but also produced in Europe, was also popular in the eighteenth century for men's and boys' clothing (Montgomery, 308).

Silk: Silk was in use at the end of the eighteenth century in New England even in the new settlements, but only a few of the finest families in town would have had silk garments. The silk materials that were in use in the early 1790s for women's gowns and men's suits were plain taffetas and lustrings (a crisp, lightweight silk), satins, and fabrics with woven-in stripes, delicate sprigs or small geometric designs. References to particular colors are found in the section on The Open and the Round Gown in Part 2. Generally light colors and small-scale designs were typical of the late eighteenth century (Smithsonian, 11).

Linen and Wool: Linen was produced everywhere (Hunter, 141). Most households put some land into flax; the tiresome process of turning the cut stems into fiber, preparatory to spinning, was done in the winter evenings when other farm chores were not in progress. Wool was also produced and spun at home, and many women did spinning for other households as a cottage industry (Goodrich, 72).

Butternut bark was used for dyeing, but the most common dyestuff for homespun yarn and cloth was indigo. Several accounts mention that the indigo tub was placed in the chimney corner in the autumn, to keep it warm. Covered with a board, it formed a "cosy seat" for a visitor, particularly a young man courting one of the daughters of the family. But indigo prepared for dyeing has an unpleasant odor, and accidentally overturning the indigo tub was a minor disaster for the visitor. "Nothing so roused the indignation of thrifty housewives, for besides the ignominious avalanche of blue upon the floor, there was an infernal appeal made to another sense than sight" (Goodrich, 65). Once a "clothiers" mill was established in a town, some of the homespun and home-woven woolen cloth could be dyed and finished commercially, giving a finer grade of cloth and a greater variety of color. A glossy wool cloth called "calamanco" was used for petticoats, gowns and men's suits.

Today, the natural fiber fabrics tend to be more expensive than their synthetic counterparts. This may seem to be reason enough to make reproduction clothing from a polyester-cotton blend or acetate satin material. But using modern materials to reproduce eighteenth-century clothing may yield an unsatisfactory result when the finished garment refuses to look quite "real" enough. The synthetic fabrics tend to be shinier and more resilient than the natural ones, and do not handle or drape the same, just as vinyl, urethane or synthetic suede do not behave like their leather counterparts. Striking the right balance among authenticity, price, availability and ease of care will be a personal decision.

For people who want to experiment with natural fiber fabrics and real garment leather, Part 4 of this book contains some sources, and others may be found in the advertisements in the backs of sewing magazines. It is also worth rummaging in remnant stores and in drapery and upholstery supply houses, which may have just the right piece of material at just the right price. There are also skilled spinners and weavers throughout New England who maintain the techniques and the interest necessary to make reproduction fabrics, and who will weave fabrics to order. Some of these craftspeople also advertise in the various specialty sewing and weaving magazines, or may be located through state crafts centers, weavers' guilds or local crafts schools. And at least one school — the Marshfield School of Weaving — teaches even total beginners how to spin and weave using eighteenth-century techniques.

The Basics of Hand Sewing

Eighteenth-century clothing was made with just a few basic hand sewing stitches. Of course, reproduction garments can be sewn by machine, but the hand stitches are given here for those who would like to know how it was done, or like to try the experience of sewing by hand. (One of the interpreters at Plimoth Plantation was asked by a visitor, "Do you sew all your clothes by hand?" She replied, "How else? That is as if I was asked, 'do I eat by mouth?'")

Oversewing: This is a method for joining pieces at the woven edge of the fabric (the selvage or selvedge), without causing a raised or bumpy seam which could chafe. It was used for piecing fabric for shifts and shirts, and for joining narrow pieces of linen together to make sheets. It is important not to pull the stitches either too tightly (or the seam will pucker and not lie flat) or too loosely (or the two joined edges will overlap and make a ridge).

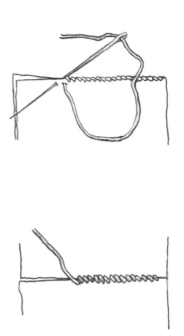

First, hold the two pieces to be joined with their right sides together and their selvages lined up (or baste or pin them into position). Starting on one end, sew over and over through the first thread or two of both selvages, keeping the successive stitches parallel to one another and just a few threads apart. When the seam is done, open it out so the two selvages lie flat, next to each other. The machine-stitch equivalent would be to hold the selvages edge-to-edge as they pass into the machine, and to use a wide zig-zag or mending stitch with a short stitch length to sew the pieces together.

Stitching (counted-thread backstitching): This is basic stitch for sewing seams. In some old garments, this stitch looks very much like machine stitching. This was done by marking and measuring the stitching by the weave of the material being stitched, just as counted-thread embroidery is still done today. If the seam was a straight one, as were all the seams on shirts and shifts, a thread of the material was pulled out where the seam was to go, to serve as a marking line for stitching. Pulling a thread also has the effect of making room for the line of backstitching to sink into the fabric being sewn, so that it almost becomes invisible. Curved seams were marked with a line of basting stitches in a contrasting color.

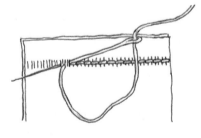

After the thread has been pulled, hold or baste or pin the two pieces together. If the stitch length is to be three threads long, first make one starting stitch three threads long by starting at one end of the seam, sticking in the needle, and bringing it out again three threads ahead. Then go back and stick the needle in again where you started. All the rest of the stitches will be formed the same way, but will progress along the seam. Bring the needle out this time six threads ahead of where it was stuck in. Next, go back and stick it in again three threads back, exactly where it was pulled out in the formation of the previous stitch. Repeat this method to the end of the seam. The machine stitch equivalent, of course, is a simple straight stitch.

Hemming: First, turn under the raw edge, and then fold for the hem. Sew with

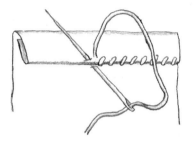

slanting stitches which pick up a few threads of the material beyond the folded edge, and come out up through the folded edge of the hem.

Seam Finishes: By and large, eighteenth-century garments are not as finely finished inside as one might expect from their outside appearance. Very tightly woven silks, for example, whose cut edges would not ravel, were often left raw or just finished with a pinked edge (cut in a zig-zag pattern with a special tool). Highly "dressed" or fulled wool cloth also would not ravel (like the boiled wool familiar today) and could be left with unfinished edges. Edges which involved a selvage of the material did not need to be finished.

A garment with a lining was finished, at the edges where the lining met the outer fabric, by turning the seam allowance of the lining toward the outer fabric and turning the seam allowance of the outer fabric toward the lining. The resulting sandwich was either stitched through all four layers, or was overcast along the edge. Where a folded-over piece, such as a cuff or a collar, was attached to a plain or gathered raw edge, such as the end of a sleeve, the raw edge was inserted into the pocket formed by the folded-over piece. Then, either each side was hemmed down, or the whole sandwich was stitched through all five layers.

For seams which could ravel, three finishes were used. In one method, both seam allowances were folded to one side and caught down to the fabric with catch or "cat" stitches. This was often used for light silks. In the second method, the seam allowances were spread open and each side caught down (twice as much catch-stitching, but necessary on thick woolen fabrics).

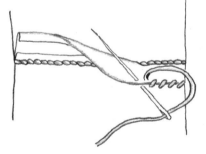

The third method, used when the material would be subject to hard wear and much washing, is the flat seam or the felled seam (known today as the flat-fell seam). A wider seam allowance is necessary for this method. After the seam is sewn, turn the two seam allowances to one side, trim the underneath one, and then turn under the edge of the top seam allowance and hem it to the fabric.

Gathering: The technique called "stroked" gathering can reduce a surprising length of material to a very small space. Take small, even running stitches straight across the grain of the piece to be gathered, by counting the threads. Then pin the end of the material to a cushion and push the material up the gathering thread, using the blunt end of the needle to stroke into the groove formed by each stitch, so that the gathers lie evenly next to one another as they are drawn up the thread.

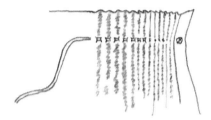

To attach the gathered piece to a plain one, sew over and over (as in the instructions for "oversewing"), but taking one overcasting stitch into the fold of each tiny gather. This technique is used whether the gathered edge is attached to a finished edge or is encased by another folded-over piece such as a collar or cuff.

Topstitching: Unlike modern machine topstitching, hand topstitching does not form a continuous line. Eighteenth-century topstitching is done with a "prickstitch," in which a small stitch shows on the outside of the fabric, followed by a space about three stitches in length, followed by another stitch. The decorative effect is of a series of evenly spaced indentations along the edge of the fabric or seam.

Sewing leather: The traditional Abenaki method for sewing leather involved the use of specially prepared sinew (tendon) for stitching, with an awl for making the holes in the leather. The settlers sewed leather with waxed linen thread, also with an awl. There are many books available on leather craft techniques, and some of the catalogues that supply leather for clothing also provide booklets on how to sew with leather.

Part 4

Resources

Full-Size Patterns

Patterns from all the companies listed below (except for Doering Designs) are stocked by Amazon Drygoods, 2218 E. 11th St., Davenport, IA 52803-3760, and by Campbell's, P.O. Box 400, Gratz, PA 17030-0400, or may be ordered from the individual companies. Write for current cost of these companies' catalogs.

Doering Designs, Rt. 2, Box 43; Dassel, Minnesota 55325 carries a full line of "Nordic-style" patterns, adapted with modern sewing techniques from Norwegian and Swedish traditional costumes. Only the men's vest would be useable without alteration, but the breeches (called "knickers") could be altered by adding more fullness to the seat. The sewing instructions are very clear, and Doering Designs also carries Norwegian cast pewter buttons and eyelets which might be useful in eighteenth century reproductions.

Eagle's View Patterns, 706 Riverdale Road, Ogden, Utah 84405 has a full line of "early American" patterns, of which I have only seen the men's shirt and waistcoat patterns. The waistcoat would be useable if shortened, but the shirt has an inappropriate curved neck seam and faced front slit opening. From the catalogue description of a "full gathered seat," it is possible that the "broadfall drop front breeches" from this company would be appropriate. It is difficult to say anything about the women's clothing from the pattern catalog alone, but the bodice does not appear to give the correct shape.

Folkwear Patterns has an eighteenth-century quilted petticoat pattern, as well as an Empire-style dress. The patterns are now available through The Taunton Press, 63 S. Main St., Box 5506, Newtown, CT 06470-5506.

A series listed in the Amazon catalog simply as "Eighteenth Century Patterns" seems to show the patterns from Green River Forge, P.O. Box 715, Roosevelt, Utah 84066. I have not worked with these patterns, but from the drawings in the catalogue, the "high waisted breeches" and the "early American shirt" appear to be correct for this time period.

Old World Patterns, Route 2, Box 103; Cold Spring, Minnesota, 56320 carries an 1805 Empire gown.

Past Patterns, 2017 Eastern, S.E.; Grand Rapids, MI 49507, which carries the widest variety of accurate historic patterns, has not to date produced any patterns earlier than about 1820, but they are always producing new ones.

Pegee of Williamsburg (in the Campbell's and Amazon catalogs) has a full line of 1776 patterns. The men's coat and breeches may provide a good starting point, but again, it is difficult to say anything from the drawings about the women's gown.

Period Impressions (in the Campbell's and Amazon catalogs) carries an 1809 gown with the type of fitted back shown in the chemise gown illustration in this book, but with a high empire waistline in front.

Kathleen B. Smith (see next section) and Amazon Drygoods also carry a set of reduced scale pattern diagrams from the Royal Ontario Museum. Series 2 covers the period 1780-1800.

Mail-Order Fabric, Thread, Leather and Stockings

Kathleen B. Smith Textile Reproductions, P.O. Box 48, West Chesterfield, MA 01084; (413) 296-4437. Supplies textile goods for historic clothing and furnishings, including fabrics, tapes and threads of wool, silk, cotton and linen; buttons; books; sewing and needlework tools. Catalog and swatches available; write for current fee schedule.

Natural Fiber Fabric Club, 521 Fifth Avenue, New York, NY 10175. Annual membership fee. Catalog of basics, plus quarterly seasonal selections and mailings of sales from time to time.

G Street Fabrics Mail Order Service, 12240 Wilkins Ave., Rockville, MD 20852. Will send swatches on request. Write for fee schedule.

Thai Silks, 252 State Street, Los Altos, CA 94022. Wide variety of silks, some cottons. Note: "Thai" silk with warp and weft in different colors is the "changeable" or "shot" silk mentioned in this book.

Utex Trading Enterprises, 710 Ninth Street, Suite 5; Niagara Falls, NY 14301. Wide variety of silks.

Martha Pullen Co., Inc., 518 Madison St., Huntsville, Alabama 35801. Focus is on French hand sewing and smocking of children's dresses. Carries several grades of Swiss cotton batiste which may be suitable for chemise gowns and fashionable neckerchiefs and aprons.

Testfabrics Inc., P.O. Drawer O, 200 Blackford Ave., Middlesex, NJ 08846. Wide variety of undyed cottons, linens, silks and wools. Good source for white material for shifts, shirts, neckerchiefs, aprons, chemise gowns.

YLI Corporation, 45 West 300 North, Provo, Utah 84601. Silk sewing thread and narrow silk ribbon.

Things Japanese, 9805 N.E. 116th St., Suite 7160; Kirtland, WA 98034. Silk filament thread suitable for use in sewing machines (two weights, many colors).

DMC Corporation, 107 Trumbull St., Elizabeth, NJ 07206. Cotton embroidery and sewing thread.

Tandy Leather Company, P.O. Box 2934, Fort Worth, TX 76113. Everything needed to sew garments and moccasins from leather, plus books and information on some types of beadwork.

Grey Owl Indian Craft Co., Inc., 113-15 Springfield Blvd., P.O. Box 507, Queens Village, NY 11429. In business for over 40 years carrying an enormous variety of Native American crafts supplies, books, recordings and information.

The Vermont Country Store, Mail Order Office, P.O. Box 3000, Manchester Center, VT 05255-3000. Carries, among many other things, cotton lisle knee socks and tights, and some cotton yard goods.

Instruction and Information:

Costume:
The Costume Society of America -- National: 55 Edgewater Drive, P.O. Box 73, Earleville, Maryland 21919; Region I (New England and the Eastern Provinces): 79 Brookville Ave., Brockton, MA 02402.

The Circle of the Rose -- Newsletter for re-enactors and others interested in historic clothing. 79 Brookville Ave., Brockton, MA 02402

Dance:
The Green Mountain Volunteers, 354 North Street, Burlington, VT 05401.

Vocal Music:
The Bayley-Hazen Singers, R.D. 1, Box 668, Plainfield, VT 05667.

Weaving:
The Marshfield School of Weaving; Plainfield, VT 05677

Part 5

Bibliographies:

Books and Periodicals - Primary Sources

Books and Periodicals - Secondary Sources

Paintings, Prints and Drawings

Costume Pieces in Museum Collections

Books and Periodicals—Primary Sources

This section includes travel writings, diaries and reminiscences of people who lived during the time period covered by this book, even if those reminiscences are contained as selections in anthologies or town histories edited or compiled at a later date.

"Manners and Customs of Olden Time." Collections of the New Hampshire Historical Society V (1837): 225-228

Armstrong, Laural. "Born 1806 - reminiscences written in 1850's about Dorset Vermont." In Humphrey, Zephine, The Story of Dorset, 137-139. Rutland, VT: The Tuttle Co., 1924.

Ballard, Martha Moore. "Mrs. Ballard's Diary." In Nash, Charles Elventon, The History of Augusta, 229-464. Augusta, ME: Charles E. Nash & Son, 1904.

Bascom, Ruth Henshaw. Diary, 1789-1846. In American Women's Diaries from the Collection of the American Antiquarian Society; New Canaan, CT: Readex Film Products, 1984. Microfilm.

Beecher, Lyman. Autobiography, correspondence, etc. of Lyman Beecher, edited by Charles Beecher. New York: Harper & Bros., 1865.

Brissot, J.P. New Travels in the United States of America, performed in 1788. London: J.S. Jordan, 1794.

Churchill, Amos. "Something Concerning the General Customs of the People 60, 50 and as late as 40 Years Ago," (written in 1853) s.v. "Town of Hubbardton." In Vermont Historical Gazetteer, Vol. III, 760-763, ed. Abby Maria Hemenway. Claremont, NH: The Claremont Mfg. Co., 1877

Cutting, Nathaniel. "Extracts from a Journal of a Gentleman visiting Boston in 1792." Proceedings of the Massachusetts Historical Society, Vol. 12 (1871-73): 60-67.

de St. Mery, Moreau. American Journey, 1793-1798, translated and edited by Kenneth Roberts and Anna M. Roberts. Garden City, N.Y.: Doubleday & Co., Inc., 1947.

Dwight, Timothy, [Jr.]. Travels in New-England and New-York. New Haven: by the author, 1821-22.

Emery, Sarah Anna. Reminiscences of a Nonagenarian. Newburyport, MA: William H. Huse & Co., 1879.

Felt, Joseph B. The Customs of New England. Boston: Press of T.R. Marvin, 1853.

Goodhue, Rev. Josiah F. History of the Town of Shoreham, Vermont. Middlebury, VT: By the town, 1861.

Goodrich, Samuel Griswold. Recollections of a Lifetime. New York and Auburn: Miller, Orton & Co., 1857.

Hadfield, Joseph. An Englishman in America, 1785, edited by Douglas S. Robertson. Toronto: The Hunter-Rose Co., Ltd, 1933.

Heath, Elizabeth. "Extracts from the Journals and Letters of Miss Betsey Heath." In Crafts, James Monroe. The Crafts Family. Northhampton, MA: Gazette Printing Co., 1893.

Hollister, Hiel. Pawlet for One Hundred Years. Albany, NY: J. Munsell, 1867; reprint, Pawlet, VT: Pawlet Historical Society, 1976.

Hubbell, Seth. A Narrative of the Sufferings of Seth Hubbell & Family, in his beginning a settlement in the town of Wolcott, in the state of Vermont. Danville, VT: E. & W. Eaton, Printers, 3rd ed. 1826.

Hunter, Robert, Jr. Quebec to Carolina in 1785-1786, edited by Louis B. Wright and Marion Tinling. San Marino, CA: The Huntington Library, 1943.

Joslin, J., B. Frisbie and F. Ruggles. A History of the Town of Poultney, Vermont. Poultney, VT: Journal Printing Office, 1875.

Lee, Lucinda. Journal of a Young Lady of Virginia (1787). Richmond, VA: Robert E. Lee Memorial Assn., Inc., n.d.

Mussey, [June] Barrows, ed. We Were New England: Yankee Life by Those Who Lived It. New York: Stackpole Sons, 1937.

Neal, John. Wandering Recollections of a Somewhat Busy Life. Boston: Roberts Bros., 1869.

Perkins, Nathan. A Narrative of a tour through the State of Vermont from April 27 to June 12, 1789, by the Rev. Nathan Perkins of Hartford. Woodstock, VT: The Elm Tree Press, 1920.

Reynolds, Sir Joshua. "Discourse VII" (1776), in Eighteenth-Century English Literature, edited by Geoffrey Tillotson, Paul Fussell, Jr., and Marshall Waingrow, 1220. New York: Harcourt Brace & World, Inc., 1969.

Shippen, Nancy. Nancy Shippen: Her Journal Book, compiled and edited by Ethel Armes. 1935; reprint, New York and London: Benjamin Blom, 1968.

Smith, Helen Evertson. Colonial Days and Ways, As Gathered from Family Papers. First published in 1900; reprint, New York: Frederick Ungar Publishing Co., 1966.

Steele, Zadock. The Indian Captive. Montpelier, Vt: by the author, 1818.

Thompson, D.P. History of the Town of Montpelier. Montpelier, VT: L.P. Walton, 1860.

Tyler, Mary Hunt Palmer. Grandmother Tyler's Book: The Recollections of Mary Palmer Tyler, 1775-1866. Edited by Frederic Tupper and Helen Tyler Brown. New York and London: G.P. Putnam's Sons, The Knickerbocker Press, 1925.

Weeks, John Moseley. History of Salisbury, Vermont, edited by G.A. Weeks. Middlebury, VT: A.H. Copeland, 1860.

Wells, Frederic P. History of Newbury, Vermont. St. Johnsbury, VT: The Caledonian Co., 1902.

Williams, J.C. The History and Map of Danby, Vermont. Rutland, VT: McLean & Robbins, 1869.

Winslow, Anna Green. Diary of Anna Green Winslow: A Boston School Girl of 1771. edited by Alice Morse Earle. Boston and New York: Houghton, Mifflin and Co., 1894.

Books and Periodicals—Secondary Sources

Andersen, Ellen. Moden i 1700-årene [Styles of the 18th Century]. Copenhagen: Nationalmuseet, 1977.

Arnold, Janet. Patterns of Fashion 1: Englishwomen's dresses & their construction c. 1660-1860. first published 1964. New edition London and Basingstoke: Macmillan London Ltd., 1977; reprinted New York: Drama Book Publishers, 1989.

Baumgarten, Linda. Eighteenth-Century Clothing at Williamsburg. Williamsburg, VA: The Colonial Williamsburg Foundation, 1986.

Bernstein, Alice. Masterpieces of Women's Costume of the 18th and 19th Centuries, New York: Crown Publishers, 1959.

Bishop, Robert. Folk Painters of America. New York: E.P. Dutton, 1979.

Boucher, François. 20,000 Years of Fashion: The History of Costume and Personal Adornment. New York: Harry N. Abrams, Inc., 1987

Bradfield, Nancy. Costume in Detail: Women's Dress 1730-1930. Boston: Plays Inc. 1968.

Braun-Ronsdorf, Margarete. Mirror of Fashion: A History of European Costume, 1789-1929. New York and Toronto: McGraw-Hill Book Company, London:Thames and Hudson, 1964. Translation of Modische Eleganz: Europäische Kostümgeschichtel von 1789- bis 1929. Munich: Verlag Georg D.W. Callwey, 1963.

Brett, K.B. Women's Costume in Early Ontario. Toronto, Ontario: University of Toronto, Royal Ontario Museum, 1966.

Brink, Jeanne. Conversations with author in January - March, 1990. Graduate student in Native American Studies, Norwich University, Montpelier, VT.

Brooklyn Museum. Of Men Only: A review of Men's and Boys' Fashions, 1750-1975. New York: Brooklyn Museum, 1976.

Bruhn, Wolfgang and Max Tilke. A Pictorial History of Costume. New York and Washington: Frederick A. Praeger, 1955.

Bryant, Nancy O. "Buckles and Buttons: An Inquiry Into Fastening Systems Used on Eighteenth Century English Breeches." Dress, Vol. 14 (1988):27-38.

Buck, Anne. "The Countryman's Smock." Folk Life vol. I (1963): 16-34.

Buck, Anne. Dress in Eighteenth-Century England. New York: Holmes & Meier Publishers, Inc., 1979.

Burnham, Dorothy K. Cut My Cote. Toronto: Royal Ontario Museum, 1973.

Callister, J. Herbert, compiler. Dress from Three Centuries: Wadsworth Athaneum. Hartford: Wadworth Athaneum, 1976.

Calloway, Colin G. The Abenaki. (Indians of North America Series - general editor, Frank W. Porter III). New York and Philadelphia: Chelsea House Publishers, 1989.

Cassin-Scott, Jack. Costume and Fashion in Color, 1760-1920. London: Blandford Press Ltd. and New York: The Macmillan Company, 1971.

Clark, Charles E. The Eastern Frontier. New York: Alfred A. Knopf, 1970.

Collard, Eileen. Early Clothing in Southern Ontario. Burlington, Ontario: by the author, 1969.

Colle, Doriece. Collars,...Stocks,...Cravats: A History and Costume Dating Guide to Civilian Men's Neckpieces, 1655-1900. Emmaus, PA: Rodale Press, Inc., 1972.

Craigie, Sir William A. and James R. Hulburt, eds. A Dictionary of American English on Historical Principles. Chicago: University of Chicago Press, 1938.

Crawford, Mary Caroline. Social Life in Old New England. Boston: Little, Brown, and Co., 1914.

Cunnington, C. Willett and Phyllis Cunnington, Handbook of English Costume in the 18th Century. London: Faber and Faber, 1957.

Cunnington, Phyllis. Costume in Pictures. London: Studio Vista Limited and New York: E.P. Dutton and Co., 1964.

Day, Gordon. Field notes from research collected 1957-1977. In the collection of the author, Canadian Ethnology Service, Hull, Quebec. Photocopy.

de Dillmont, Thérèse. Encyclopedia of Needlework. New Edition. Mulhouse (Alsace): D.M.C. and Boston: The Modern Pricilla, n.d.

De Pauw, Linda Grant and Conover Hunt. Remember the Ladies, Women in America, 1750-1815. New York: The Viking Press, 1976.

Earle, Alice Morse. Two Centuries of Costume in America: 1620-1820. New York: The Macmillan Company, 1903; reprinted Rutland, VT: Charles E. Tuttle Co., 1971.

Ettesvold, Paul M. The Eighteenth Century Woman. New York: The Metropolitan Museum of Art, 1981.

Ewing, Elizabeth. Dress and Undress: A History of Women's Underwear. New York: Drama Book Specialists, 1978.

Fairbanks, Edward T. The Town of St. Johnsbury, Vermont. St. Johnsbury: The Cowles Press, 1914.

Fennelly, Catherine. Textiles in New England, 1790-1840. Sturbridge, MA: Old Sturbridge Village, 1961.

Fennelly, Catherine. The Garb of Country New Englanders, 1790-1840. Sturbridge, MA: Old Sturbridge Village, 1966.

Fenwick, Carroll. The Goldsbury Family. Unpublished manuscript drawn from family history and letters in the Archives of Barre History, Aldrich Public Library, Barre, VT, n.d.

Fiske, Patricia L., ed. Imported and Domestic Textiles in 18th-Century America (Irene Emery Roundtable on Museum Textiles, 1975 Proceedings). Washington, DC: The Textile Museum, 1976.

Frankenstein, Alfred and the editors of Time-Life books. The World of Copley: 1738-1815. Time-Life Library of Art series. Alexandria, VA: Time-Life Books, 1970.

Gehret, Ellen J. Rural Pennsylvania Clothing, Being a Study of the Wearing Apparel of the German and English Inhabitants, both men and women, who resided in Southeastern Pennsylvania in the late Eighteenth and Early Nineteenth Century. York, PA: Liberty Cap Books 1976.

Goodyear, Frank H., Jr. American Paintings in the Rhode Island Historical Society. Providence: The Rhode Island Historical Society, 1974.

Grølsted, Esther. Everyday Clothes in the Country, Summer 1788. Copenhagen: Nationalmuseet, 1988.

Hall, Benjamin H. History of Eastern Vermont. N.Y.: D. Appleton & Co. (1858).

Harrowven, Jean. The Origins of Rhymes, Songs and Sayings. London: Kaye and Ward, 1977.

Haviland, William A. and Marjory W. Power. The Original Vermonters: Native Inhabitants, Past and Present. Hanover, NH and London: University Press of New England for University of Vermont, 1981.

Hicks, Marjorie, compiler. Clothing for Ladies and Gentlemen of Higher and Lower Standing: A working pamphlet to aid the imitators of New England citizens of the eighteenth century. Minute Man National Historic Park, Mass., National Park Service, U.S. Department of the Interior, 1976.

Hileman, Gregor. "The Iron-willed Black Schoolmaster and his Granite Academy." Middlebury College News Letter 48 (Spring 1974):6-14.

Hill, Margot Hamilton and Peter A. Bucknell. The Evolution of Fashion: Pattern and Cut from 1066 to 1930. London: B.T. Batsford Ltd., 1967 and New York: Van Nostrand Reinhold Company, 1968.

Hollander, Anne. Seeing Through Clothes. New York: The Viking Press, 1978.

Horsman, Reginald. The Frontier in the Formative Years, 1783-1815. New York: Holt, Rinehart & Winston, 1970.

Houde, Cornelia H. Frisbee. Not Just Another Pretty Dress: Two Centuries of Clothing and Textiles from Cherry Hill. Albany, NY: Historic Cherry Hill, 1982.

Hunnisett, Jean. Period Costume for Stage and Screen: patterns for women's dress 1500-1800. London: Bell & Hyman, 1986.

Jaffe, Irma B. John Trumbull, Patriot-Artist of the American Revolution. Boston: New York Graphic Society, 1975.

Johnson, Mary Moyars, with Judy Forbes and Kathy Delaney. Historic Colonial French Dress: A Guide to Re-creating North American French Clothing. W. Lafayette, IN: Ouabache Press, 1982.

Kerber, Linda K. Women of the Republic: Intellect and Ideology in Revolutionary America. Chapel Hill, NC: Published for the Institute of Early American History and Culture, Williamsburg, VA, by the University of North Carolina Press, 1980.

Kidwell, Claudia B. "Riches, Rags and In-between." Historic Preservation, 28 No. 3 (July-Sept. 1976).

Kidwell, Claudia. "Short Gowns." Dress, Vol. 4 (1978):30-65.

Klinger, Robert L. Distaff Sketch Book. Union City, TN: Pioneer Press, 1974.

Klinger, Robert L. Sketch Book '76. Union City, TN: Pioneer Press, 1967.

Kornhauser, Elizabeth Mankin, with Richard L. Bushman, Stephen H. Kornhauser, and Aileen Ribeiro. Ralph Earl: The Face of the Young Republic. New Haven and London: Yale University Press in association with the Wadsworth Atheneum, Hartford, 1991.

Larkin, Jack. The Reshaping of Everyday Life, 1790-1840. New York: Harper & Row, 1988.

Laver, James and Iris Brooke. English Costume of the Eighteenth Century. New York: Barnes and Noble, 1931.

Ludlum, David M. Social Ferment in Vermont, 1791-1850. New York: Columbia University Press, 1939, reprinted 1966 AMS Press, Inc.

Maeder, Edward. "The Elegant Art of Dress" in An Elegant Art: Fashion and Fantasy in the Eighteenth Century. New York and Los Angeles: Los Angeles County Museum of Art in Association with Harry N. Abrams, Inc., 1983.

McClellan, Elisabeth. Historic Dress in America, 1607-1870. First published 1904; reprint New York: Arno Press, Inc., 1977.

Merrimack Valley Textile Museum. All Sorts of Good Sufficient Cloth: Linen-Making in New England, 1640-1860. North Andover, MA: Merrimack Valley Textile Museum, 1980.

Miller, Maria Stephens. "A Case Study of a Unique Eighteenth Century Gown Belonging to the University of North Carolina at Greensboro Collection." M.S. thesis, University of North Carolina, 1989.

Montgomery, Florence M. Textiles in America, 1650-1870. New York: W.W. Norton & Co., 1984.

Moody, John. "The Native American Legacy" in Always in Season: Folk Art and Traditional Culture in Vermont, edited by Jane C. Beck. Montpelier, VT: Vermont Council on the Arts, 1982.

Moore, Doris Langley. Fashion Plates, 1771-1970. New York: Clarkson & Potter, Inc., 1971.

Murray, Anne. "From Breeches to Sherryvallies." Dress, Vol 2 (1976):16-33.

Myers, Annie E. Home Dressmaking: A complete guide to Household Sewing. Chicago: Charles H. Sergel & Co., 1892.

Oakes, Alma and Margaret Hamilton Hill. Rural Costume, Its Origin and Development in Western Europe and the British Isles. London: B.T.Batsford, Ltd. 1970.

Opie, Iona and Peter, eds. The Oxford Dictionary of Nursery Rhymes. Oxford: The Clarendon Press, 1951, reprinted with corrections, 1952.

Ribeiro, Aileen. A Visual History of Costume: The Eighteenth Century. London: B.T. Batsford Ltd. and New York: Drama Book Publishers, 1983.

Ribeiro, Aileen. Dress in Eighteenth Century Europe, 1715-1789. New York: Holmes & Meier, 1984.

Ribeiro, Aileen. Fashion in the French Revolution. New York, Holmes & Meier, 1988.

Richardson, Edgar P., Brooke Hindle, and Lillian B. Miller. Charles Willson Peale and His World. New York: Harry N. Abrams, Inc. for The Barra Foundation, 1983.

Sadik, Marvin. Christian Gullager: Portrait Painter to Federal America. Washington, DC: National Portrait Gallery, Smithsonian Institution, 1976.

Sellers, Charles Coleman. "Portraits and Miniatures by Charles Willson Peale." Transactions of the American Philosophical Society 42, part 1 (1952).

Severn, Bill. The Long and Short of It: Five Thousand Years of Fun and Fury over Hair. New York: David McKay Company, Inc., 1971

Shine, Carolyn R. "Scalping Knives and Silk Stockings: Clothing the Frontier, 1780-1795." Dress, Vol. 14 (1988):39-47.

Simpson, Ruth M. Rasey. Hand-Hewn in Old Vermont. Bennington, VT: By the author, 1979.

Sizer, Theodore. The Works of Colonel John Trumbull, Artist of the American Revolution. New Haven and London: Yale University Press, 1967.

Smith, Barbara Clark. After the Revolution: The Smithsonian History of Everyday Life in the Eighteenth Century. New York: Pantheon Books and the National Museum of American History, 1985.

Smithsonian Institution, "Getting Dressed: Fashionable Appearance, 1750-1800" Script and label text from Costume Study Gallery in the Exhibition "After the Revolution: Everyday Life in America 1780-1800," National Museum of American History, Smithsonian Institution, Washington, DC. Photocopy. Unnumbered - my page numbering.

Sprague, Laura Fecych, ed. Agreeable Situations: Society, Commerce and Art in Southern Maine, 1780-1830. Kennebunk, ME: The Brick Store Museum, 1987.

Sprigg, June. Domestick Beings. New York: Alfred A. Knopf, 1984.

Swan, Susan Burrows. Plain and Fancy: American Women and Their Needlework, 1700-1850. New York: Rutledge Book/ Holt, Rinehart, Winston, 1977.

The Undercover Story. New York: Fashion Institute of Technology, 1982, and Kyoto: Kyoto Costume Institute, 1983.

Thieme, Otto Charles. Simply Stunning: 200 Years of Fashion from the Cincinnati Art Museum. Cincinnati: Cincinnati Art Museum, 1988.

Tierney, Tom. American Family of the Early Republic: Paper Dolls in Full Color. New York: Dover Publications, Inc., 1988.

Tozer, Jane and Sarah Levitt. Fabric of Society: A Century of People and their Clothes, 1770-1870. Carno, Powys, Wales: Laura Ashley Ltd., 1983.

Tucker, William Howard. History of Hartford, Vermont. Burlington, VT: The Free Press Assn., 1889.

Wallace, Carol McD., Don McDonagh, Jean L. Druesedow, Laurence Libin, and Constance Old. Dance: A Very Social History. New York: The Metropolitan Museum of Art and Rizzoli International Publications, Inc., 1986.

Warwick, Edward and Henry C. Pitz. Early American Costume. New York and London: The Century Co., 1929.

Warwick, Edward, Henry C. Pitz and Alexander Wycoff. Early American Dress: The Colonial and Revolutionary Periods. New York: Bonanza Books, 1965.

Waugh, Norah. The Cut of Men's Clothes, 1600-1900. New York: Theatre Arts Books, 1964.

Waugh, Norah. The Cut of Women's Clothes, 1600-1930. New York: Theatre Arts Books, 1968.

Waugh, Norah. Corsets and Crinolines. London: B.T. Batsford Ltd., 1970.

Wells, Daniel White and Reuben Field Wells. A History of Hatfield, Mass. Springfield, Mass: F.C.H. Gibbons, 1910.

Wilbur, C. Keith. The New England Indians. Chester, CT: The Globe Pequot Press, 1978.

Wilcox, R. Turner. Five Centuries of American Costume. New York, Charles Scribner's Sons, 1963.

Wilcox, R. Turner. The Dictionary of Costume. New York: Charles Scribner's Sons, 1969.

Wilcox, R. Turner. The Mode in Hats and Headdress. New York: Charles Scribner's Sons, 1945.

Williams, Hermann Warner, Jr. Mirror to the American Past: A Survey of American Genre Painting: 1750-1900. Greenwich, CT: New York Graphic Society, 1973.

Worrell, Esther Ansley. Early American Costume. Harrisburg, PA: Stackpole Books, 1975.

Paintings, Prints, and Drawings

This is not by any means an exhaustive list of portraits and genre scenes from this time period.

Ames, Ezra. Self-Portrait. Gouache on ivory. ca. 1790. Albany Institute of History and Art, Albany, NY.

[The Beardsley Limner]. Mrs. Hezekiah Beardlsey (Elizabeth Davis). Oil on canvas. 1785-90. Yale University Art Gallery, New Haven, CT.

-----. Mrs. Oliver Wight (Harmony Child). Oil on canvas. 1786-93. Old Sturbridge Village, Sturbridge, MA.

-----. Oliver Wight. Oil on canvas. 1786-93. Old Sturbridge Village, Sturbridge, MA.

Brewster, John, Jr. Colonel Thomas Cutts. Oil on canvas. ca. 1795-1800. Dyer-York Library and Museum, Saco, ME.

-----. Mrs. Thomas Cutts (Elizabeth Scamman). Oil on canvas. ca. 1795-1800. Dyer-York Library and Museum, Saco, ME.

-----. James Eldredge. Oil on canvas. n.d. Connecticut Historical Society, Hartford, CT.

----- (attributed). Lucy Gallup Eldredge. n.d. Connecticut Historical Society, Hartford, CT.

Chandler, Winthrop. Captain Samuel Chandler. Oil on canvas. National Gallery of Art, Washington.

-----. Mrs. Samuel Chandler. Oil on canvas. National Gallery of Art, Washington.

Copley, John Singleton. Midshipman Augustus Brine. Oil on canvas. 1782. Metropolitan Museum of Art, New York.

-----. The Copley Family. Grisaille study. ca. 1789. Museum of Fine Arts, Boston.

-----. Winslow Warren. Oil on canvas. ca. 1790. Museum of Fine Arts, Boston.

David, Jacques Louis. Antoine Laurent Lavoisier and His Wife. Oil on canvas. 1788. Metropolitan Museum of Art, New York.

Earl, James. Mehitable Knight Dexter. Oil on canvas. 1794-95. Rhode Island School of Design.

-----. Mrs. William Mills (Rebecca Pritchard) and her daughter Eliza Shrewsbury. Oil on canvas. 1794-96. Winterthur Museum, Winterthur, DE.

-----. Elizabeth Fales Paine and her Aunt. Oil on canvas. 1794-96. Rhode Island School of Design.

Earl, Ralph. Samuel Burr. Oil on canvas. n.d. Connecticut Historical Society, Hartford, CT.

-----. Dr. David Rogers. Oil on canvas. 1788. National Gallery of Art, Washington.

-----. Martha Tennet Rogers and Daughter. Oil on canvas. 1788. National Gallery of Art, Washington.

-----. Daniel Boardman. Oil on canvas. 1789. National Gallery of Art, Washington.

-----. Elijah Boardman. Oil on canvas. 1789. Private collection, reproduced in Montgomery, Textiles in America (frontispiece).

-----. Mrs. Benjamin Tallmadge with her son and daughter. Oil on canvas. 1790. Litchfield Historical Society, Litchfield, CT.

-----. Mrs. William Taylor. Oil on canvas. 1790. Albright-Knox Art Gallery, Buffalo, NY.

-----. Mrs. William Moseley (Laura Wolcott) and son Charles. Oil on canvas. 1791. Yale University Art Gallery, New Haven, CT.

-----. Mrs. Richard Alsop. Oil on canvas. 1792. National Collection of Fine Arts, Washington.

-----. Chief Justice and Mrs. Oliver Ellsworth. Oil on canvas. 1792. Wadsworth Athaneum, Hartford, CT.

-----. Angus Nickelson family. Oil on canvas. ca. 1792. Museum of Fine Arts, Springfield, MA.

-----. Mrs. Joseph Wright. Oil on canvas. 1792. National Collection of Fine Arts, Washington.

-----. Huldah Bradley. Oil on canvas. 1794. Museum of Fine Arts, Boston.

-----. Mrs. N. Smith and Children. Oil on canvas. 1798. Metropolitan Museum of Art, New York.

Eckstein, Johann. The Samuels Family. 1788. Museum of Fine Arts, Boston.

Gullager, Christian. Jeremiah Williams. Oil on canvas. ca. 1789-90. National Museum of American Art.

-----. Mathilda Davis Williams. Oil on canvas. ca. 1791-92. National Museum of American Art, Washington.

Hathaway, Rufus. Lady with her Pets (Molly Wales Leonard). 1790. Metropolitan Museum of Art, New York.

----- (attributed). Mrs. Ezra Weston, Jr. (Jerusha Bradford). Oil on canvas. ca. 1793. Abby Aldrich Rockefeller Folk Art Center, Williamsburg, VA.

Jennys, Richard (attributed). Mrs. Ashbel Baldwin (Clarissa Johnson). Oil on canvas. n.d. Connecticut Historical Society, Hartford, CT.

----- (attributed). Hannah Lewis Hitchcock. Oil on canvas. n.d. Connecticut Historical Society, Hartford, CT.

Johnston, John. Man in a Grey Coat. Oil on canvas. ca. 1788. Museum of Fine Arts, Boston.

Krimmel, John L. Village Tavern. Oil on canvas. ca. 1813-14. Toledo Museum of Art, Toledo, OH.

Peale, Charles Willson. Benjamin Rush. Oil on canvas. 1783. Winterthur Museum, Winterthur, DE.

-----. The Accident on Lombard Street. Etching on paper. 1787. Winterthur Museum, Winterthur, DE.

-----. William Smith and His Grandson. Oil on canvas. 1788. Virginia Museum, Richmond, VA.

-----. The Children of Benjamin Stoddard. Oil on canvas. 1789. The National Society of the Colonial Dames of America.

-----. Robert Goldsborough Family. Oil on canvas. 1789. Private Collection. Reproduced in Richardson, Hindle & Miller, 214-15.

-----. Mrs. Robert Milligan (Sarah Cantwell Jones) and her daughter Catherine Mary. Oil on canvas. 1791. Winterthur Museum, Winterthur, DE.

_____. David Rittenhouse. Oil on canvas. 1791. American Philosophical Society, Philadelphia.

-----. James Madison. Oil on canvas. ca. 1792. Thomas Gilcrease Institute of American History and Art, Tulsa, OK.

-----. Charles Pettit. Oil on canvas. 1792. Worcester Art Museum, Worcester, MA.

-----. Exhuming the Mastodon. Oil on canvas. 1806-08. The Peale Museum, Baltimore.

Peale, James. The Artist and His Family. Oil on canvas. ca. 1795. Pennsylvania Academy of Fine Arts, Philadelphia.

Savage, Edward. The Washington Family. Oil on canvas. 1796. National Gallery of Art, Washington.

[The Sherman Limner]. Portrait of a Lady in Red. ca. 1785-90. National Gallery of Art, Washington.

-----. Portrait of a Man in Red. ca. 1785-90. National Gallery of Art, Washington.

Steward, Joseph (attributed). Rebecca Stillman Burr. Oil on canvas. n.d. Connecticut Historical Society, Hartford, CT.

Stuart, Gilbert. Henrietta Elizabeth Frederica Vane. Oil on canvas. 1782-83. Smith College, Northampton, MA.

-----. James Heath. Oil on canvas. ca. 1785. Wadsworth Athaneum, Hartford, CT.

-----. Miss Vick and her cousin, Miss Forster. Oil on canvas. 1787-92. Private collection. Reproduced in Swan, Plate 10.

-----. Luke White. Oil on canvas. ca. 1790. National Gallery of Art, Washington.

-----. Betsy Hartigan. Oil on canvas. ca. 1793. National Gallery of Art, Washington.

-----. Mrs. Richard Yates (Catherine Brass). Oil on canvas. 1793-94. National Gallery of Art, Washington, DC.

Trumbull, John. Alexander Hamilton. Oil on canvas. ca. 1792. National Gallery of Art, Washington.

Vigee-Lebrun, Elisabeth. Portrait of A Lady. Oil on canvas. 1789. National Gallery of Art, Washington.

West, Benjamin. The Old George Inn. Oil on canvas. 1796. Private collection. Reproduced in Williams, Mirror to the American Past.

Wright, Joseph. John Jay. 1786. New York Historical Society, New York.

-----. Self and Family. 1793. Pennsylvania Academy, Philadelphia.

Unknown artists:

Possibly English:

-----. Forty-Nine Watercolor Fashion Paintings. 1784-1805. Shelburne Museum, Shelburne, VT. Accession Number 27.2.6-18 (Numbered 1 to 50 (missing No. 25)).

American:

-----. Daniel Bullard. Pastel on paper. ca. 1790. Winterthur Museum, Winterthur, DE.

-----. Mrs. Silas Casey. Oil on canvas. ca. 1790. Society for the Preservation of New England Antiquities.

-----. Oliver Crosby. Pastel on paper. ca. 1790. Winterthur Museum, Winterthur, DE.

-----. Sally Bullard Crosby. Pastel on paper. ca. 1790. Winterthur Museum, Winterthur, DE.

-----. Catherine Cuyler. Oil on canvas. ca. 1790. Albany Institute of History and Art, Albany, NY.

-----. The Domino Girl. Oil on canvas. ca. 1795

-----. Mrs. Ruth Stanley Mix. Oil on canvas. 1788. Abby Aldrich Rockefeller Folk Art Center, Williamsburg, VA.

-----. Quaker Meeting. ca. 1790. Museum of Fine Arts, Boston.

-----. Timothy Swan. Oil on canvas. ca. 1795. American Antiquarian Society.

-----. Dr. Philemon Tracy. Oil on canvas. ca. 1790. National Gallery of Art, Washington.

French:

-----. Pierre Samuel du Pont de Nemours. Oil on canvas. 1790-91. Winterthur Museum, Winterthur, DE.

Costume Pieces in Museum Collections

Shifts
  Barre Historical Society 64.1922.2
  Colonial Dames, Boston No.88
  Northhampton Historical Society 66.912
  Old Sturbridge Village 26.26.64 and 69
  Smithsonian Institution (Copp Family) 6730D
  Vermont Historical Society 60.180.2; 58.1.1182, 1183 and 1184.

Stays
  Chester County Historical Society, Jane Pyle, 1799
  Essex Institute, Salem, MA. 132.537 and 116.114
  Sheldon Museum, Middlebury, VT. Mrs. Martha Barto, Hinesburg, VT. 1795.
  Smithsonian Institution (Cooper-Hewitt) 311503.183
  Vermont Historical Society 43.5.1. Mrs Samuel French, Jericho, VT. 1795.

Pockets
  Noah Webster House, Hartford, CT 70.48
  Vermont Historical Society R59.37.16

Petticoats
  Boston Museum of Fine Arts 43.703
  Colonial Dames 1982 No. 72
  Essex Institute 107,303
  Essex Institute 121,280b
  Smithsonian Institution 36478; 244131.1

Open and Round Gowns
  Boston Museum of Fine Arts 43.703; 51.1968; 54.633
  Chester County (PA) Historical Society 00/76 clf 209
  Cincinnati 1938.3.
  Connecticut Historical Society 1956.45.62; 1979.68.864
  Essex Institute 101,033; 104,508
  Los Angeles County Museum of Art 81.135.2; M57.24.9; M82.122.3; M86.238; TR3630.1
  Metropolitan Museum of Art 1977.698.4
  Old Sturbridge Village 26.33.47; 26.33.60
  University of North Carolina 19.0651a,b & c
  Vermont Historical Society 77.16.1
  Wadsworth Athaneum 1973.61; 1974.1124

Shortgowns
  Chester County (PA) Historical Society 00/76 clf 189
  Connecticut Historical Society 1988-7-1
  Old Sturbridge Village 26.93.1
  Smithsonian Institution 12107

Women's Neckerchiefs
  Vermont Historical Society OCHW 86.0.14

Aprons
  Northampton (MA) Historical Society 1986.143.7

Shirts
  Barre Historical Society 64.1922.1 and 2
  Noah Webster House, 87-279

Smithsonian Institution (Copp Family) 6658A and 6680A

Vermont Historical Society 60.76.2

Men's Neckwear

Smithsonian Institution 1981.0512.09 (cravat); 15466 (stock)

Breeches

Old Sturbridge Village 26.40.21, 31, 32, 42, 43, and 44

Smithsonian Institution 18900, 15446

Vermont Historical Society 1982.26.3

Windham County (VT) Historical Society, Ebenezer Wiswall.

Waistcoats

Boston Museum of Fine Arts 02.10

Smithsonian Institution T15706

Coats

Fort Ticonderoga (NY), Phineas Jaquish

Shoes and Stockings

Smithsonian Institution 1981.0512.06 and .07 (men's shoes and buckles); 20055 (women's shoes); (Copp Family) 6550A (women's stockings); Cooper-Hewitt 311303.2 (women's shoes).

Author Merideth Wright was an environmental lawyer by profession before her appointment in November 1990 as Vermont's first environmental judge. Her life-long interest in international folk dancing led to her becoming intrigued with ethnic costume, and to her volunteer work at the Smithsonian Institution identifying a collection of Macedonian folk costumes. After moving to Vermont in 1978, her involvement with a traditional New England dance performance group, the Green Mountain Volunteers, turned her costume attention to the historic clothing of rural New England. She and her husband, son, and daughter live on top of a hill in central Vermont, from whence they carry on their daily lives, interspersed, as time and money permit, with travel near and far for international and New England folk dancing and for singing with the Bayley-Hazen Singers.

Illustrator Nancy Rexford's interest in costume began in childhood but did not take a professional turn until she became Curator of Costume at the Northampton (Massachusetts) Historical Society in 1975. Since 1978 she has worked extensively as a consultant helping museums around the United States identify and date their collections of nineteenth-century women's and children's clothing. She received grants from the National Endowment for the Humanities in 1983 and 1991 to write and illustrate Women's Clothing in America, 1795-1930, a reference work in several volumes containing detailed information both on dating garments and on the changing social rules which determined how and when clothing was worn. The first volume (on shoes) will be published by Holmes & Meier, 30 University Place, New York, NY 10003. Later volumes will cover dresses, headgear, underwear and outerwear, and accessories such as collars, fans, and parasols.